*Starring John Wayne
As Genghis Khan*

Also by Damien Bona

Opening Shots: The Unusual, Unexpected, Potentially Career-Threatening First Roles That Launched the Careers of 70 Hollywood Stars

Inside Oscar: The Unofficial History of the Academy Awards (with Mason Wiley)

Starring John Wayne As Genghis Khan

★ ★ ★ ★ ★ ★ ★ ★ ★

HOLLYWOOD'S ALL-TIME WORST CASTING BLUNDERS

DAMIEN BONA

A Citadel Press Book
Published by Carol Publishing Group

For Raffy

Copyright © 1996 by Damien Bona
All rights reserved. No part of this book may be reproduced in any form, except by a newspaper or magazine reviewer who wishes to quote brief passages in connection with a review.

A Citadel Press Book
Published by Carol Publishing Group
Citadel Press is a registered trademark of Carol Communications, Inc.
Editorial, sales and distribution, and rights and permissions inquiries should be addressed to Carol Publishing Group, 120 Enterprise Avenue, Secaucus, N.J. 07094.

In Canada: Canadian Manda Group, One Atlantic Avenue, Suite 105,
    Toronto, Ontario M6K 3E7

Carol Publishing Group books may be purchased in bulk at special discounts for sales promotion, fund-raising, or educational purposes. Special editions can be created to specifications. For details, contact: Special Sales Department, Carol Publishing Group, 120 Enterprise Avenue, Secaucus, N.J. 07094.

Manufactured in the United States of America
10 9 8 7 6 5 4 3 2 1

Library of Congress Cataloging-in-Publication Data

Bona, Damien, 1955–
    Starring John Wayne as Genghis Khan : Hollywood's all-time worst casting blunders / Damien Bona.
        p.   cm.
    "A Citadel Press book."
    ISBN 0-8065-1797-2 (pbk.)
    1. Motion picture actors and actresses—Casting—United States.
PN1995.9.C34B66   1996b
791.43′028′092273—dc20   95–48048
                                                            CIP

Contents

WAXWORKS

*The most unconvincing portrayals of historical figures
ever captured on film*

THE RACE CARD

*Ethnic impersonations that might well have set race relations
back decades. Who needs verisimilitude
when you can have a movie star?*

GENERATION GAP

*Actors who refused to age gracefully on-screen, and one
who was in too much of a hurry to grow old*

AN ERROR IN ERAS

*Performers whose personas and modern sensibilities
were completely out of place when they traveled to the past*

OUT OF THEIR LEAGUE

*Movie stars whose attempts at roles different than those
they usually played were stymied by either
a too strongly established screen persona
or simply by limited acting skills*

CITY SLICKERS

A trio of actors who did not look at home on the range

MEDIEVAL MISFITS

Actors who convinced us chivalry is indeed dead

HOW WE WON THE WAR

*Some unlikely spies in the battle against Hitler
and the Axis powers*

DON'T GIVE UP THE DAY JOB

*Three men—of varying talents—from the world of pop music
who were at sea when playing against type
in rare film appearances*

KNOTTED FAMILY TIES

Family trees that produced some very strange fruit

THE MISCASTING HALL OF FAME

*Three actors who, despite undeniable
talent and a portfolio of fine performances, also spent
a good portion of their careers way over their heads*

Acknowledgments

It never ceases to amaze me how many people are involved in the writing of a book, and my deep thanks go out to all those who helped me in so many ways.

No one could ask for more supportive parents than my mother, Alma, and my late father, Arthur, and I'll always be extremely grateful to them. Thanks also to my sister, Amy Bona, brother-in-law, Neil B. Cohen, and very cool nieces, Emily, Elizabeth, and Claudia Bona-Cohen, for love and encouragement.

It was difficult and sad to work on a book without having my close friend and frequent collaborator, Mason Wiley, around. How I miss calling him with arcane questions, being the beneficiary of his insights and knowledge, turning to him for support, and, most of all, hearing his laughter. But Mason's spirit, nevertheless, infuses this book, and there were so many times I could hear him telling me to watch out for run-on sentences, to find another synonym for *miscast* and to not be mean to Barbra.

My terrific agent and friend, Lynn Seligman, was true to form: savvy, tireless, and full of good cheer. At Carol Publishing, thanks to my editors Carrie Nichols Cantor and Bruce Shostak, and designer Anne Ricigliano. Thanks also to copy editor Al Marill.

Bill Condon and Ryan Murphy should have their pictures in the dictionary next to *generous* (and, for that matter, *gracious* and *bighearted*). Their help on this project has truly been immeasurable. Similarly, it's great to know I could turn to Joe Smith for any number of reasons; his friendship has been a marvelous gift for over two decades.

I would wish for every writer a stalwart like Steve Garland: his enthusiasm is lavish; his benevolence, boundless; and his joyfulness, infectious. I am indebted to Spencer Beckwith and Frank Pike for reading drafts of the manuscript, sharing their smarts and ensuring that I kept on track; even they are not fully aware of how important their help was. They're also a great font of information on subjects ranging from E. M. Forster to Charlie Callas.

Lori Solinger is an incomparably inspiriting friend; her frequent phone calls from Rhode Island to check in on me were a wonderful tonic. And it's been great having Bob Montgomery in my corner since the days of John Jay Hall at Columbia.

Because of the marvelous staff, it's a pleasure to do research at the Billy Rose Theatre Collection of the Lincoln Center Library for the Performing Arts. Thank you, David Bartholomew, Rod Bladel, Patricia A. Darby, Donald W. Fowle, Christopher Firth, Don Glenn, Christine Karatnytsky, Louise M. Martzinek, Brian O'Connell, Daniel C. Patri, Louis Paul, Mary Ellen Rogan, Rosalie Spar Sacks, Edward J. Sager, Betty Travitsky, Kevin Winkler, and Barbara Worrell-Purdue. The same is true of the Margaret Herrick Library of the Academy of Motion Picture Arts and Sciences, and my gratitude goes to the gang there: Director Linda Mehr, Joe Adamson, Val Almendarez, Sandra Archer, Laurie Asa-Dorian, Stacey Behlmer, Doug Bell, Rusell Butner, Mei Chen, Anne Coco, Scott Curtis, Robert Cushman, Pat DeFazio, Lisa Epstein, Mark Frerking, Lisa Gall, Steve Garland, Harry Garvin, Sam Gill, Russell Good, Tony Guzman, Barbara Hall, Grafton Harper, Lisa Jackson, Lynne Kirste, Gary Krause, Kristine Krueger, Don Lee, Janet Lorenz, Davis Marsh, Tina McKenzie, Scott Miller, Karl Neimoller, Frans Offermans, Susan Oka, Howard Prouty, Kathryn Reesman, Lucia Schultz, Naomi Selfman, Warren Sherk, Mary Anne Thomas, Faye Thompson, Jonathan Wahl, Greg Walsh, Dan Woodruff, and, of course, my old friend, Carol Cullen.

Thanks to Mary Corliss and Terry Geekson of the Museum of Modern Art Still Collection, and Howard and Ron Mandelbaum and the staff at Photofest, who made gathering photos the easiest part of this book.

And my deep appreciation goes out to all of the following for aiding and abetting in myriad ways: The Ryans—Rob, Shelley, Louisa, and Shelley Jr.; Josephine Peña; Mark Sullivan and Elizabeth Terhune; Paul Maggio; Esteban Chalbaud; Jim Nugent; Howard Karren and Ed Christie; Ed Sikov; Genie Leftwich; Dallas Murphy; Susan Ross; Julia Pearlstein; Dick Beebe; Ina Rose; Yong Soon Min and Allan de Souza; Bridget Fonger; Jason Pomerance and Sam Destro; Tom Rhoads; Bruce Finlayson; Jane Croes; Rosanna Arce; Honey and Bob Hilzen; Emily and Irv Fistolera; Tom Phillips and Ed Davis; Ron Fried and Lorraine

Kreahling; Andy Dickos; George Robinson; Ira Hozinsky; Margaret Perry; Rhoda Penmark; Gilbert Cole; Helen Wiley and Marian Payson; Shirley Cohen; Marty Cohen; Jay Kenny; Kevin Winkler; Sandy Donnelly, Ann and Nick Vitale; Margaret and John Galasso; Dale Tucker; Lee Alan Morrow; Nora Presutti; Susie Day; Marie Marsham; Gerry Khosravanlou; Dare Clubb; Doug Culhane; Sara Smarr; Lynn Kotula; Susan Davis; Rick Freyer; Horace Bogardus; Mark Gaylord; Steve Stark; Kathleen Haspel; Jonathan Powell; Luke Henry; Paul Richmond; Sheldon Garber; Emily Lester; Dr. Nancy Schnur; Angie DeVito; and Tiffany the Cat, who stayed up into the wee small hours to keep me company while I wrote.

And the person whom I needed most on this book, Ralph Peña.

Introduction

If someone happens to mention Genghis Khan, is an image of John Wayne the first thing that pops into your head? Unfortunately, it *was* for Dick Powell, the producer of *The Conqueror*, the deliriously awful epic about the Mongolian barbarian's exploits.

Did someone actually think that the quintessentially American Gary Cooper, with his flat speaking voice, could pass muster as Venetian Marco Polo, or that Jack Palance had the stuff of a Fidel Castro impersonator? That TV star James Brolin possessed the same charisma that made Clark Gable the "King of Hollywood"? The answer to all of the above questions is yes, and the results are some of the most absurd moments in film history.

It wasn't, however, only with these impersonations of real-life people that Hollywood expertise seemed to go haywire. A tenet of the movies' studio era was that audiences would plunk down their money to see their favorite stars on screen, and it didn't much matter what roles they were playing. That explains why Alan Ladd, of all people, fought heroically for King Arthur in *The Black Knight* and how it came to pass that Katharine Hepburn put a little tape around her eyelids and pretended she was a Chinese peasant in *Dragon Seed*.

But casting miscalculations did not disappear with the death of the studio system—recent times have seen any number of doozies. There's Melanie Griffith in Germany doing undercover work against the Nazis in *Shining Through*, Tom Hanks straining to be imperious as Sherman McCoy in *The Bonfire of the Vanities*, sexpot Sharon Stone making like a frigid wife in *Intersection*, and Michael Keaton as a Batman to make you root for the bad guys. Not to mention Dustin Hoffman pretending to be the son of Sean Connery and the father of Matthew Broderick in *Family Business* a year after trying to pass himself off as Tom Cruise's brother in *Rain Man*.

What was going on here? These mismatchings of actor and role first had to be approved by a whole phalanx of people: producers, directors, studio executives, the actors themselves. Wasn't there an agent or assistant vice president at the studio or a spouse who might have said, "Now wait a minute, fellas!"? Wouldn't it have seemed that at least one person involved in the production of *The Mission* might have said, "No, Al Pacino does not belong in colonial America?" Mightn't a gaffer on the set of *The Pride and the Passion* have suggested that no one was going to buy Frank Sinatra as a Spanish freedom fighter—during the Napoleonic Wars, no less?

Miscasting is a tricky business, though. No one would have mistaken James Stewart for a resident of Germany or Hungary, and yet the gawky young man from Pennsylvania gave beautiful performances under those guises in *The Mortal Storm* and *The Shop Around the Corner*. Most times when a Caucasian actor plays a member of a different race, the results are stultifying. But Luise Rainer is as luminous as Katharine Hepburn is ludicrous, portraying a Chinese peasant (in *The Good Earth* and *Dragon Seed*, respectively). Then there are those cases in which the casting was intended to be outrageous. Mickey Rooney is a wildly stereotypical Japanese photographer in *Breakfast at Tiffany's*, a performance which people have been known to find offensive. But the theme of the film is that love is the only safe harbor in a world that is insane. By presenting us with a universe in which *Mickey Rooney* is Japanese, director Blake Edwards has certainly created a crazy world. Thus, on one level, Rooney is badly miscast, on another, his presence works wonderfully well. (But then there's Mickey Rooney as Lorenz Hart . . .)

This book presents sixty-nine movie stars at their worst. Whether it's Tony Curtis's Bronx accent showing up in sixteenth-century England or Elvis running an inner-city health clinic and falling hard for Mary Tyler Moore, who happens to be a nun, or Humphrey Bogart as a zombie-vampire hybrid, these are actors performing without a clue.

To be *mis*cast, an actor has to have spent the bulk of his or her career *well* cast—he can't really be wrong for a role until he has established a personality strong enough to mark him as ill suited for it. (As for singers Tony Bennett and Johnnie Ray, they had formed readily identifiable personas through their music. And though it is his first movies that are explored here, Walter Matthau was already an established personality on the New York stage.) All of the actors covered in this book have done good work—at least during some part of their careers. (Okay, maybe not Patrick Swayze, but everybody else.) Watching actors under these circumstances makes you much more appreciative of their sterling performances in other movies—seeing them miscast and without a clue makes you realize what they were capable of, and it isn't pretty.

Why is it so enjoyable to see well-known movie stars looking this ridiculous? In part, it's reassuring to have concrete evidence that nobody is perfect, not even Marlon Brando. Plus, watching an out-of-place performer is just plain fun. In life, if you can't laugh at yourself, whom can you laugh at? Miscast actors.

WAXWORKS

*The most unconvincing portrayals of historical figures
ever captured on film*

William Bendix

The Babe Ruth Story (1948)

"Little Leaguer"

The most famous sports star of all time, Babe Ruth can be seen in a number of movies, joking, laughing, even occasionally breaking into song. In these films, he's a total charmer who exhibits a vibrant joie de vivre. The one word that best describes him is jaunty. By contrast, William Bendix, throughout his career, combined a hulking body with the personality of a (usually) good-natured, not-too-bright, blue-collar Everyman, epitomized by his starring role in *The Life of Riley* on radio and TV. The term "lovable lug" comes to mind.

The lead character of *The Babe Ruth Story* is more William Bendix than Babe Ruth, but little in this movie bears resemblance to reality of any kind. Sportswriters, nightclub operators, and fast women of the day knew there was an enormous dichotomy between the Babe's public image and his personal life. To most Americans, the Yankee slugger was a sentimentalist who loved to have fun, play with dogs, and hang out with kids—heck, he was just a big kid himself. Away from the newsreel cameras, however, the exalted Babe turned profane: a hard-drinking, womanizing carouser whose exploits would have horrified parents, teachers, and clergymen everywhere—certainly the antithesis of William Bendix, who stayed married to the same heavy-set plain-Jane from the old neighborhood his entire life.

Given the tenor of the 1940s and the fact that its hero was still alive, it is not surprising that *The Babe Ruth Story* ignores the ballplayer's dissolute side. What is remarkable is the degree to which director Roy

If Babe Ruth had had a batting stance like William Bendix's, he never would have gotten out of AA ball.

Del Ruth and writers Bob Considine and George Callahan further embellish the standard cock-and-bull version of his life; the movie contains so much maudlin humbug that it barely gives us even the Babe Ruth of myth.

This is the film's version of Babe Ruth: The Sultan of Swat hits a dog with a line-drive foul at Comiskey Park. Grief-stricken, he hightails it to a hospital with the injured mutt (which has the tug-at-your-heartstrings name Pee-Wee) and its inconsolable, freckle-faced young owner. But Ruth isn't quite bright enough to know that animals have special doctors, called veterinarians. When told that "We only operate on humans," he responds, "What's more human than this little pooch?" Such childlike innocence can't help but move the sawbones, who ignores his patients in order to bring the mutt back to life.

But the Ruth of this movie doesn't only save animals, not when there are sickly little boys waiting to be cured. A simple "Hi" from the Babe, or a personally delivered baseball, and the lame can walk, the dying are revived. *The Babe Ruth Story* chronicles almost as many miracles as *King of Kings*. At the end of the film, the parallels between Babe Ruth and Jesus Christ become even more overt, as the ballplayer shows a willingness to lay down his life for others. He agrees to become the guinea pig for a potentially deadly serum, developed, wouldn't you know it, by the same doctor who saved Pee-Wee the dog those many years ago. If this medicine works, it can also be prescribed for millions of other invalids. William Bendix musters all the considerable bathos at his disposal, agreeing to the experiment because, "It's a swell world. There's a lot of swell people in it."

William Bendix hardly resembled Babe Ruth. In an attempt at marginal verisimilitude, the actor's hair was darkened and he was given a putty nose, which merely served to make his profile look like Cyrano de Bergerac's. Hi Phillips of the *New York Sun* wrote a poem entitled "To Bill Bendix": "You're a damned good actor/But to tell the truth/I look like Citation/If you look like Babe Ruth."

Bendix plays the character as a wide-eyed dope, although a dope with a heart as big as the great outdoors. In his ill-conceived portrayal, the towering figure of Ruth is made simplistic and stupid. Others considered for the role were Orson Welles, Paul Douglas, and, most logically, Jack Carson, but Bendix makes Ruth such a dolt that they might as well have cast Lou Costello. In reality, Ruth had a surprisingly lilting voice and a slight Southern accent redolent of his Baltimore birthplace; Manhattan-born Bendix speaks with a gruff New York accent. Babe Ruth swaggered, Bendix oozes sincerity. Ruth was boisterous and self-assured, Bendix plays him as a sheepish oaf. Bendix also appears absolutely ill-at-ease in the baseball scenes (despite the fact that as a youngster he worked as a club-house boy, turnstile boy, and bat boy at the Polo Grounds, then the home of both the New York Giants and the Yankees, and later played in the minor leagues) and doesn't even begin to approximate Ruth's unique batting stance and swing. John McCarten of the *New Yorker* snorted that Bendix "handles a bat as if it were as hard to manipulate as a barrel stave." And in the scenes showing Ruth as a pitcher, Bendix, as they used to say in the schoolyard, throws like a girl. Bendix was a large man, Ruth was larger than life. The main difference between the two is that while William Bendix was likable but not terribly charismatic, the real Babe Ruth was charismatic but not terribly likable.

The Babe Ruth Story was excoriated by the press. The *Los Angeles Daily News* complained, "We can't believe that the Babe was ever so mushy or that there was anywhere nearly so much hokum as is represented in this picture." As dreadful as the film is, Babe Ruth was such a beloved and seminal American icon that the movie actually did quite nicely at the box office—it managed to outgross such well-regarded concurrent releases as *The Treasure of the Sierra Madre, A Double Life*, and *Kiss of Death*.

At the end of the film, the Babe is—as the scenarists of the piece might have put it—down to his last strike. He is last seen being wheeled down a hospital corridor to try out that mysterious serum, and when the film wrapped shooting no one knew what the final outcome would be. As it turned out, Ruth was still around when *The Babe Ruth Story* opened. He left the hospital to attend the premiere with his wife but, in the course of watching what Hollywood had done to him, suffered a relapse. Three weeks later he was dead.

James Brolin and Jill Clayburgh

Gable and Lombard (1976)

"Pretenders to the Throne"

One shouldn't come down too hard on James Brolin and Jill Clayburgh for their performances in *Gable and Lombard*. Nobody could have been seen to good advantage under these circumstances. What they need to be castigated for is their hubris in thinking they could approximate two incomparable movie stars. And they *were* punished for the sin of pride: *Gable and Lombard* was a near unanimous choice as one of the worst films of not only 1976 but the entire decade.

In Barry Sandler's script, the two characters named Clark Gable and Carole Lombard bear at most a passing resemblance to their real-life counterparts. Gable was a highly ambitious young man: very aware of his sex appeal, he readily serviced (and was serviced by) whoever he thought might help him in his career. Antithetically, the film's hero is baffled at finding himself a movie star and has a take-it-or-leave-it attitude toward his fans' adulation. Despite his reputation as a man's man, Gable had little interest in *Field and Stream* activities until the studio publicity machine forced him outdoors to shoot skeets and ride horses, the better to live up to the image moviegoers wanted to have of him. The Gable of *Gable and Lombard*, however, is a sheepish, shambling, "aw shucks" kind of guy who was more at home on the range than at a table at Ciro's. (A typical comment from this Gable is "Holy jumpin' catfish!") It's as though the only research material writer Sandler and director Sidney J. Furie turned to were old MGM press releases.

If *Gable and Lombard* neuters Clark Gable, it does just the opposite to Carole Lombard. Having heard about her reputation for salty language, Sandler turns Lombard into a lowlife vulgarian. By most accounts,

Frankly, my dear, they don't look a damn bit like Carole Lombard and Clark Gable.

she had as much class off the screen as on, but the film's facsimile is a trollop who chatters endlessly about getting laid. Her version of whispering sweet nothings to Gable is "What are you waiting for, you big ape? Get your pants off!" You know that they're in love because they're forever insulting each other, playing practical jokes, and brawling. They're the kind of loud, self-involved couple you would ask the flight attendant to move you away from on a plane.

His mean wife won't give him a divorce, and what passes as plot in *Gable and Lombard* is how, because of the mores of the time, the two of them cope with having to be furtive lovers. Gable is disgusted by the hypocrisy of it all and feels that they should consider "giving up all this movie star crap for a chance to just be ourselves." There's also a fictitious paternity suit thrown in, with Lombard saving the day by proudly proclaiming that on the night he supposedly sired the baby, he was in bed with her. The worst aspect about this crass enterprise is its smarminess about the pair's sexual relationship—all you need to know about the quality of *Gable and Lombard* is that Carole Lombard is shown to be so fixated on her lover's penis that she knits it a stocking cap.

Gable and Lombard turned out to be such a bungle—and so thoroughly wrong-headed a project—that it's surprising to realize that, prior to its release, the film was a big deal. Universal had tried to rekindle memories of *Gone With the Wind* by creating a publicity campaign over who should play the duo. Columnist Joyce Haber solicited casting suggestions from her readership. Robert Redford was the public's first choice for Gable, followed by David Janssen (who, because of his own jug ears, always harbored suspicions that Gable was his father). Respondents mustn't have been too familiar with Carole Lombard because the top vote-getters were Barbra Streisand and Faye Dunaway. Among those suggested by people who were either wiseacres or morons: Robert Blake and Diahann Carroll.

Although James Brolin, best known for his TV supporting role on *Marcus Welby, M.D.*, had sought the part of Gable from the outset, Universal wanted Burt Reynolds, who passed. There was talk of Steve McQueen, but the studio lost interest when he insisted that his own Carole Lombard, Ali MacGraw, also be cast. Warren Beatty would only consider the picture if the lead characters' names were changed, which sort of defeated the purpose. Director Sidney J. Furie claimed never to have seen James Brolin in *Marcus Welby, M.D.*, but cast him after catching him do a guest stint on *The Sonny Bono Comedy Review*, which should have been an omen.

During production, Brolin said that he didn't want to do a straight imitation of Clark Gable because "that would be campy." Watching Gable's movies, Brolin picked up on "a musical way in his speech. He had something like an Italian inflection, a way of ending his words and sentences rhythmically." Another actor with an instantly identifiable voice must also have had that musicality, because the person Brolin most resembles vocally in *Gable and Lombard* is Walter Brennan. On-screen, Gable was effortlessly self-assured; Brolin tries so hard to be natural that his awkwardness makes you feel sympathy pains. Physically, there's a fair resemblance to his real-life counterpart from some angles, none at all from others. The biggest distinction between the prototype and the copy is that Gable's twinkling eyes have been replaced by a quizzical gaze that borders on the imbecilic.

Overtaking early front-runners Valerie Perrine and Sally Kellerman, Jill Clayburgh was a semi-known up-and-coming actress when she landed *Gable and Lombard*. She resembled Carole Lombard not in the least (as thirties movie comediennes go, she looked more like Jean Arthur), nor did she have Lombard's breathy vocal quality. Clayburgh's task was not as formidable as Brolin's simply because the public did not have as strong an image of Lombard as they did of Gable. Yet she still manages to give an awful performance. Mannered and shrill, Clayburgh simply lacks the effervescence that flowed so naturally from the real article.

Despite all the scorn that was heaped upon *Gable and Lombard* ("cheap, vulgar and inane," declared *Newsweek*'s Jack Kroll), Clayburgh emerged relatively unscathed. Toward the end of the seventies she had a brief stint as a big-time leading lady, until her self-satisfied drabness got on everybody's nerves. James Brolin had hoped that *Gable and Lombard* would be his ticket out of television. ("I hate television," he stated in 1974. "All it does is sap energy from actors." At the time the movie was released, he was, in fact, suing to get out of his contract for *Marcus Welby*, saying that the series prevented him from being taken seriously as an actor.) But because *Gable and Lombard* was followed by such dillies as *The Car* and *Capricorn One*, Brolin eventually returned to the small screen. Nevertheless, he has never tried to make excuses for *Gable and Lombard*, even claiming to be proud of his effort. A decade later he told an interviewer, "I've had people come up to me at the supermarket and whisper, 'I liked *Gable and Lombard*.' But they won't say it out loud."

Gary Cooper

The Adventures of Marco Polo (1938)

"Italian Baloney"

We may not know exactly what Marco Polo's physical characteristics were, but it's a safe bet that the thirteenth-century trader and world traveler scarcely resembled Gary Cooper. Cooper looked like what he was—an upper-middle-class young man from Helena, Montana. When he opened his mouth, what emerged was not the melodiousness of the Italian language but a hesitant drawl straight out of the western United States. And as for the actor's physical rigidity and stilted body language: aren't Italians supposed to be exuberant and emotional, punctuating their remarks with grandiose hand gesticulations? (Yes, this is ethnic stereotyping, but isn't that what you expect in a film from the thirties?)

Gary Cooper starred in *The Adventures of Marco Polo* for the simple reason that this was a very expensive production and Sam Goldwyn wasn't about to cast anyone other than his biggest box-office draw. (Not that the producer had any better choices: his other leading men were David Niven and Joel McCrea.) As it turned out, *The Adventures of Marco Polo* was such a complete folly that Cooper's inappropriateness was merely one of a whole series of blunders. Frank S. Nugent of the *New York Times* tallied the number of clashing accents from the actors portraying Italians, Chinese, Tartars, and Saracens in the film, coming up with eight—and that was just among the nine top-billed actors. (Adding to the zaniness, Goldwyn was hyping leading lady Sigrid Gurie, who tossed a Norwegian timbre into the mix even though she was playing the daughter of Kublai Khan, as the most exciting Scandinavian actress since Garbo. "The Siren of the Fjords" was one appellation studio publicists

As Venetian-native Marco Polo, Montana's Gary Cooper learns about spaghetti from a Chinese scholar who is really London-born H. B. Warner.

concocted for her. During production, word got out that Goldwyn's new find was actually a native of Flatbush, Brooklyn.)

Nobody connected with this film quite knew what to make of it. Was this supposed to be a history lesson or a lighthearted romp? Pulitzer Prize–winning playwright Robert E. Sherwood seemed to be having a high old time playing hob with expectations for *The Adventures of Marco Polo*; the prologue to the film, describing the many accomplishments of this great adventurer, adds, "He was also the world's first traveling sales-man." Director John Cromwell was completely flummoxed about this project. A sober sort, he cudgeled his brains over why a script about an important real-life personage would contain dialogue that sounded like it was from a modern bedroom comedy. And what was all that screwy action stuff out of a Saturday matinee serial? Cromwell fled the production after a week. His would-be replacement, William Wyler, went on unpaid suspension rather than become involved with *The Adventures of Marco Polo*. Journeyman Archie Mayo, who had directed the film version of Sherwood's allegorical drama *The Petrified Forest*—which presented the playwright in a completely different mood—stepped in.

Goldwyn himself seemed to be at a loss. During filming, a reporter asked, "Is it true that you've tried five different endings to *Marco Polo* and can't find a good one?" "It's not the ending that's troubling us," confessed the producer. "We can't find a good beginning!" The middle was pretty bad, too. The problem is that while Robert Sherwood set about to write a facetious epic, he didn't make it very funny. Nor did he follow through on his theme, for although large chunks of *The Adventures of Marco Polo* are played for laughs, there is still much that is out of a straightforward boys' adventure. What the movie does not have is anything approximating an accurate portrayal of its titular hero. The only thing that rings true about the film's Marco Polo is that he learns about spaghetti in China, although the real traveler probably didn't mistake the pasta for snakes, as Gary Cooper does.

Just as the movie has a hybrid feel to it, Cooper's characterization is wildly inconsistent. One moment he's a romantic matinee idol, next he's a swaggering action hero, then he's a farceur, finally he's a wide-eyed naif, a Candide in China. His guises are entirely discrete, however. Unlike swashbuckler Errol Flynn, whose humor, gallantry, and romanticism were all of a piece, Cooper here never displays more than a single character trait at a given time. Even within each mode, he's erratic—as a lover, for instance, he's alternately sheepish, cocky, roguish, and poetic. The one constancy is how stiff Cooper is for the entire running time. With the right director—a Howard Hawks or an Ernst Lubitsch, who understood that there was a sensuousness beneath the actor's awkwardness—Cooper could be spectacularly good. In *The Adventures of Marco Polo*, he was pretty much left to his own devices, and it was far from his finest hour. As the old joke goes, you keep checking to see if he's sitting on Edgar Bergen's lap.

Bob Hope

Beau James (1957)

"Bogus James"

Jimmy Walker, the mayor of New York from 1926 to 1932, was a corrupt son of a bitch. He was nevertheless beloved by a large segment of the city's populace because, in an early example of the cult of personality, he had "style." Crook he may have been, but Jimmy Walker was no Richard Nixon: brooding around the hallways of Gracie Mansion and imagining enemies in the woodwork wouldn't have been for him. No, he was one of the original swingers, a man-about-town who spent his days at the ballpark and his nights at speakeasies and supper clubs, hanging out with gamblers, Broadway sharpies, and goodtime girls. Although married, the rakish mayor carried out an open affair with a showgirl—hence the nickname, the "playboy mayor."

In 1955, Bob Hope, for the first time, had played a real-life character, competently portraying vaudevillian Eddie Foy in the pleasant-enough musical biography, *The Seven Little Foys*. Having had a taste of light dramatics, he wanted more, and set his eyes on another figure from New Yorks' dear dead days. Coproduced by Hope's own company, *Beau James* cleans up Jimmy Walker's act. So much so that he becomes a fictional figure. This Jimmy Walker will tolerate no corruption. Or patronage. If he does end up playing along with the party bosses it's because he has no choice—that's the only way to get his munificent government projects off the ground.

The film would have you accept that the main reason pork barreling occurred during Walker's administration was that the good mayor was too distracted by love to notice what was going on. His estranged wife, Alexis Smith, finds his integrity a turn-off, so what choice does he have but to

13

fall into the arms of pretty chorine Vera Miles. This flagrant transgression of the Sixth Commandment gets the local Catholic church good and roiled; the boys at St. Patrick's raise a stink, spitefully endorsing the Seabury Committee, which is investigating city graft and has it sights on Walker. In actuality, the mayor resigned because the committee was closing in on him, but the movie feels it makes for a better story if he is portrayed as a selfless martyr: the celluloid Walker steps down so that those who no longer support him will not desert the Democratic party and destroy Franklin Roosevelt's chances

Would you vote for this man? Bob Hope indulges in some studied nonchalance, striking a pose as New York's "Playboy Mayor" Jimmy Walker.

of defeating Herbert Hoover in the 1932 presidential race.

Bob Hope lived for a while in Jimmy Walker's New York, having come to the city as a song-and-dance man in 1929. Back then, Hope was pretty dapper himself. He hadn't yet become "Bob Hope," but was a musical comedy performer possessing grace and dash. You can see it as late as 1938, when he sings "Thanks for the Memory" with Shirley Ross in his feature film debut, *The Big Broadcast of 1938*: Hope seems positively debonair.

Unfortunately for *Beau James*, Bob Hope in 1957 no longer possessed—at least on screen—Jimmy Walker's brand of easy-going bonhomie. Not long after Hope arrived in Hollywood, he and his writers concocted a character for him to portray: a wisecracking, leering, slightly vain, and rather cowardly go-getter; there was always something vaguely unpleasant about him. By the time he made *Beau James*, Hope's screen persona had long become calcified.

Melville Shavelson, who directed Hope in both *Beau James* and *The Seven Little Foys*, later said that "Hope liked to play down his dramatic ability. He seemed ashamed that he could act." Truth to tell, Hope had little to be ashamed of. His key acting choice in the film is repression; he holds back his natural inclination to frivol, ending up all starchy—a disastrous acting choice for playing a character who was thoroughly buoyant and breezy. But then, as if a sustained suppression of his real personality is too much to ask, he, from time to time, reverts to being Bob Hope, with all that that entails—the wisecracking, the shifty eyes, and the flippant delivery. Hope didn't look much like Walker, being taller and much stockier than the gracile mayor.

Hope's presence makes *Beau James* not simply a minor movie but a stunt: America's Favorite Funnyman gets serious. Another problem is that whenever Bob Hope appears on-screen he brings with him his long-established image of the would-be wolf who can't get to first base with women (at least not until the final reel). But in *Beau James* we have the plot turning on his involvement with a *pair* of women. It doesn't make any sense. Despite the lukewarm reception to the film, Hope later said he felt he might well have had a flirtation with a Best Actor Oscar if only someone at the studio had begun a campaign push for him.

I didn't witness Jimmy Walker's mayoralty, so the whitewashing in *Beau James* doesn't particularly bother me. But if someday there's a movie in which, say, Robin Williams portrays Ed Koch not as a strident, divisive provocateur but a funny and avuncular reconciliator, or a biography of Rudolph Guiliani (Kevin Spacey?) in which his mean-spirited bullying is transformed into the stuff of heroism, then I'll be heard from.

Jeffrey Hunter

King of Kings (1961)

"Graven Image"

Throughout the fifties, the lantern-jawed Jeffrey Hunter rivaled Robert Wagner for the title of 20th Century-Fox's resident dreamboat. Because of his pretty boy qualities, Hunter's starring role as Christ in *King of Kings* led wags to dub the film "I Was a Teenage Jesus."

Jeffrey Hunter's good looks are of a distinctively All-American variety. Christ's disciples are played by swarthy actors who look right at home in Jerusalem, and then there's Hunter with his fair skin and baby blue eyes: a Midwesterner, not a Middle Easterner. Between his flowing locks and graceful countenance, what Hunter resembles—although no such creature existed when *King of Kings* was released in 1961—is a long-haired rock star. Or a precursor to the flower children from 1967's "summer of love." To those who questioned the notion of a blue-eyed Jesus, the film's producer, Samuel Bronston, swore that several historians had assured him that "there were blue-eyed people among Palestinians in Christ's time."

The most fundamental tenet of the Christian faith is that Jesus was both God and man. In *King of Kings*, Hunter seems to be neither. His diffident performance is too namby-pamby for the human Jesus and lacks the grandeur you'd expect from God. Hunter was most likely cast because his unblemished features could be taken as a visual correlative to the purity of Jesus. But when an actor's bearing is this callow, it's impossible to accept him as a man with the ability to inspire thousands of followers.

Hunter came from Milwaukee and had the unadorned speech patterns of the heartland. One would have to assume that Jesus was a powerful orator and that, even though He spoke in accessible, everyday

As embodied by Jeffrey Hunter, Jesus predates the flower children from 1967's "summer of love."

terminology, He made use of an eloquent and dynamic speaking style. The actor recites the Sermon on the Mount with a singular lack of emotion, turning it into a laundry list of platitudes. If this is the word of God, Hunter presents it like a nonbeliever.

Bronston bragged that his star "played a marine once," adding that "Christ was a rugged man, a carpenter. He was no sissy. We play Him strong." Actually not. Generally, in such films as *The Searchers*, and *The Last Hurrah*, Hunter was an outgoing, forceful actor. But here he looks dazed. He seems intimidated by the role, as if he's afraid to give offense and wants above all to be dignified. In this film, Jesus's humanity is deemphasized to such a degree that Hunter's armpits were shaved. Hunter takes restraint to such an extent that during the entire film his face hardly moves at all; even when Christ is dying on the cross, there's nary a muscle twitch in his face. The *New York Herald-Tribune* aptly noted that Hunter

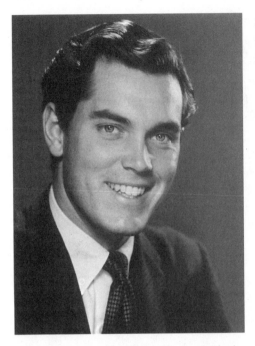

When not portraying Christ, Hunter looked like a nice young man from the accounting department.

is "relying often on a fixed stare that is not always as hypnotic as intended."

Apart from the vacuum caused by its lead actor, *King of Kings* is one of the more intelligently done films of its kind. There is almost none of the overripe dialogue one usually finds in biblical films, and while a few of the performances are jarring (in particular, Harry Guardino's Barabbas: a Burt Lancaster imitation done with a Brooklyn accent), most of the acting is of a high quality not generally associated with this genre. Credit must go to director Nicholas Ray. Naturally, *King of Kings* doesn't have the neurotic underpinnings that provide for the hauntingly febrile qualities of his greatest movies (such as *Johnny Guitar* and *Rebel Without a Cause*), but there probably has not been another biblical film in which the characters are as resonant; certainly, the Crucifixion has never been presented so effectively and with such understatement.

It's hard to believe now but *King of Kings* caused quite a commotion when it was released. *Variety* reported that "the New Testament has suddenly become New York cocktail party conversation," and chortled that this was an "unexpected dispute in which many who have never been known to attend church are among the most opinionated." Philip Yordan's script turned Barabbas, the man whose death sentence was commuted in lieu of Jesus's, into a freedom fighter against the Romans—a pioneer Zionist—although the Gospels never reveal more than that he had been arrested for murder and "a certain sedition." Yordan also attempted to make Judas into something more complex than the conventional one-dimensional apostate. Here the disciple commits his act of betrayal in the hope that, once arrested, Christ will perform miracles to save Himself, thus proving once and for all that He is God. And, in the spirit of ecumenicism, the film also downplayed the role of the Jewish Pharisees and Scribes in the death of Jesus.

The Catholic Legion of Decency didn't cotton to these liberties and assailed the film as "theoretically, historically, and scripturally inaccurate." The critic for a Jesuit newspaper, *America*, wrote that "Christ is there as a physical presence, but His spirit is absent," and griped that the filmmakers "have no opinion on the subject of Christ, except that He is a hot box-office property." On the other side of the aisle, the vicar from St. Thomas's Episcopal Chapel in New York was quoted in newspapers as taking umbrage over *King of Kings*'s "complete white-washing of the Jews," although he did allow that "Naturally, it would not do to be anti-Semitic, and it is true that Jewish responsibility for the Crucifixion can be overdone unfairly."

King of Kings provided Jeffrey Hunter with his greatest fame, but where do you go after playing Christ? His subsequent career was undistinguished, so much so that his best role post-Jesus was as a straight man in the Bob Hope–Phyllis Diller comedy *The Private Navy of Sgt. O'Farrell.*

Jack Palance

Che! (1969)

"Fidel-Sticks"

Certain Americans consider Fidel Castro to be the bête noir of the second half of the twentieth century. Years before Castro came to power, Jack Palance was already established as one of the great heavies of American movies. When Palance portrayed Castro in a motion picture, however, they both became laughable.

Che! was Darryl F. Zanuck's attempt to cash in on the messianic cult that grew around Che Guevara after the Argentine-born hero of the Cuban Revolution was killed in 1967. But even when it was trying to attract a late-sixties youth audience, 20th Century–Fox, being a capitalist American motion picture company, was not about to present a fervently committed Marxist in a favorable light. Although Zanuck and any number of other people connected with *Che!* insisted they were presenting a well-balanced portrayal, the Guevara who emerged from the movie was the Devil as left-wing guerrilla fighter. And a jerk to boot.

We're aware of Che Guevara's physical characteristics primarily from still photographs and, in his makeup, Omar Sharif looked enough like Guevara to get by. Fidel Castro, on the other hand, has been seen on the evening news for decades; the Cuban president has been in our lives for so long he's almost part of the family—we know exactly what he looks like and how he talks and how he moves. That is one reason why, while Sharif is fairly competent in *Che!*, Palance is anything but.

This movie would have you believe that Castro may have been the leader of the 1959 overthrow of despotic Cuban president Batista, but it was Che who was the brains of the outfit. *Che!* also portrays Guevara as a ruthless murderer who felt that any life was expendable for the good

With his high cheekbones, beady eyes, and angular features, Jack Palance looks less like the round-faced Fidel Castro than he does a character from *Planet of the Apes*.

of the revolution, a master propagandist who instructed Castro what to say to win the hearts and minds of Cuban peasants, and a hard-liner who saw the Soviet Union as a force for Good and who would not have been adverse to using nuclear weapons against the United States. And when he leaves Cuba to stir up things in Bolivia, he becomes even more inured to—and responsible for—human suffering.

The script shows Castro as well meaning but ineffectual. As Jack Palance portrays him, he's a buffoon. Sometimes a cigar is just a cigar, but here it is Palance's scene partner. At any given moment he's furiously working it with more abandon than Edward G. Robinson ever did. He also goes through not a bag but a steamer trunk of mannerisms: squinting and occasionally shutting his eyes, presumably deep in thought; taking long deep breaths as though weary of the whole business; slinking around Cuba, and poking the air with his finger. As a hot pitching prospect, Castro had a tryout with the New York Giants in 1949; in Palance's interpretation, he seems to be auditioning for the Actors Studio. At forty-nine, Palance was a decade too old to play the youthful man Castro was when he came to power. Despite his phony beard and mustache, you never forget that this isn't really Fidel Castro, it's Jack Palance, the movie star who terrorized Joan Crawford in *Sudden Fear* and tried to gun down Alan Ladd in *Shane*. (More than anything else, it's the beady eyes that keep reminding you of the actor's identity.) As Archer Winsten of the *New York Post* tried to explain, "Palance looks more like Castro than you would think possible. But if you accept that, he still looks more like Palance than you would think possible when he looks like Castro. And yet, the two people don't really look alike at all."

Two decades after *Che!*, Jack Palance became widely recognized as a terrific and very dry comic actor so maybe his performance as Castro was all a big put-on. Whatever the case, his is one of the more unconvincing cinematic portrayals of a contemporary world figure. If the real Fidel Castro was anything like Palance's rendition, he never would have remained in power as long as he did.

Robert Redford

Out of Africa (1985)

"Denys, Anyone?"

Conversation about *Out of Africa* centered on two things. One was Milena Canonero's beautiful period costumes, which led to a brief fad of safari chic. The other was accents: specifically, Meryl Streep's odd one and Robert Redford's lack of one. In 1985, the Meryl Streep backlash was at its zenith. No one questioned her talent, but people were, frankly, growing tired of her substituting technique for warmth. And Streep's showy insistence of nailing down every vocal nuance of far-flung characters was getting annoying. Playing *Out of Africa*'s Karen Blixen, who was better known by her pen name of Isak Dinesen, the actress went Danish. There was a good deal of mean-spirited laughter when columnist Liz Smith reported that in Blixen's native country, "Streep's accent has become something of a national joke. One TV station ran film snippets and asked viewers to call in. Most Danes agreed that Meryl sounds like she's from somewhere, but not from Denmark."

A classic overachiever, Streep may have been irritating in the manner of a straight-A student who lauds her accomplishments over her B-minus classmates, but you couldn't say that she was simply coasting. Robert Redford, on the other hand . . . first of all, Redford should never have been cast as Blixen's lover, Denys Finch Hatton, who was a nearly bald, six-and-a-half-foot-tall Englishman. But what the hey. Producer-director Sydney Pollack and Redford were pals, having worked together five other times, and what's eight inches and a head of hair between friends? Besides, Redford wasn't acting too frequently these days, so his involvement in *Out of Africa* would give the expensive movie added cachet.

In *Out of Africa*, Robert Redford was banking that his smile would make viewers forget that his character was supposed to be a bald man with a British accent.

Apparently when you've got your friend appearing in your movie, you don't worry about an accurate characterization. Denys Hatton was an upper-crust Brit, a graduate of Eton and Oxford, but Redford might as well be wearing his baseball uniform from his previous picture, *The Natural*. The dialogue that screenwriter Kurt Luedtke wrote for Hatton is in the British idiom and has the chipper quality of repartee passed back and forth at a men's club over a Pimm's cup or two. Coming from the disinterested Redford, the lines merely sound platitudinous. We forget that the character is supposed to be British—it's easy to lose sight of the fact that he's supposed to be anyone other than Robert Redford. So when, for instance, he characterizes World War I as "a silly argument between two spoiled countries," we don't think of him as a courageous man who is willing to sound seditious in speaking out against his country during a war; instead, he registers as a cranky American isolationist. Similarly, when he later refrains from joining in the singing of "God Save the King" at a New Year's Eve party, he seems less independent-minded than boorish.

There was a time when Robert Redford was an actor. Not a terribly accomplished actor, perhaps, but he was up there on the screen working hard, giving something of himself, as though he felt he had to prove that he hadn't made it solely on his looks. This time out, when he should have been dashing, he was merely laid back. He was deservedly roasted by the critics. Such comments as "a ruddy, contemporary, Midwestern type who might have made his way to Kenya in a time capsule" (*Cineaste*), a "real cipher" (*Los Angeles Times*), and "we're disgusted by him at the end" (*New York*) were his for the asking, and so well deserved.

So many other actors were around in 1985 who would have been so much more right for the role of Denys Hatton, starting with Sean Connery. Because Redford hardly seems to be on-screen, there is no rapport between him and Streep—and she's concentrating on her accent anyway.

Sydney Pollack was nothing if not loyal, for after the reviews rolled in, he swore that Redford *had* perfected a British accent, thanks to coaching from actress Jane Seymour, but that they had decided to drop it shortly before filming began because "we were worried audiences would be thrown by Bob as an Englishman." Which of course begs the question, why cast him in the first place? Pollack and Redford got away with it this time, for *Out of Africa* was a huge financial success. They eventually got theirs, though. The next time they collaborated the result was *Havana*.

Mickey Rooney

Words and Music (1948)

"Manic Depressive"

Lorenz Hart was the most glorious of all song lyricists. He was also a man who lived in torment, his anguish arising not solely from being a pre-Stonewall homosexual, but also because he was—and there is no decorous way of putting this—an ugly little man. (Hart was a romantic leading man trapped in a comic-relief body.) The lyricist was filled with self-loathing because of the gnomelike physique he felt made him repugnant to the comely young men he would have liked to have gotten to know better. His tragedy was accentuated by too much drinking, and he died at the age of forty-seven.

The mid-to-late forties saw a string of bogus biographies of composers both classical (Chopin, Schumann) and popular (Kern, Gershwin, and Cole Porter). So, typically, what did MGM go and do when it decided to produce a Rodgers and Hart musical? As dark, tortured Larry Hart, the studio cast the gee-whiz-ain't-life-swell! bundle of energy, Mickey Rooney. The only thing the two had in common was being short, although at five-foot-three Rooney still would have towered over Hart. The lyricist's despair over his height is turned into a joke in *Words and Music*, through a dopey gag in which he gains new self-esteem by purchasing elevator shoes. Hart also spoke in unadulterated New Yorkese; in the film, his mother, played by Jeanette Nolan, has a generic Eastern European accent while Mickey Rooney talks like Mickey Rooney.

The prologue for *Words and Music* beings with Tom Drake pretending to be Richard Rodgers claiming that because success came early and easily to Larry Hart and himself, their story lacks the conflicts found in the biographies of other composers. *Au contraire*: an unvarnished account of Hart's life would have made for pretty harrowing drama, only no 1948 movie could have gotten away with presenting it. The lyricist had been dead for only five years when *Words and Music* was made, so he was not such a remote figure that the film could gloss over *all* the facts of his life. It would have to acknowledge in some way the difficulties between the two songwriters, which were brought about mainly by Hart's morose self-destructiveness. But to deal with Hart's unfulfilled sexual life, writers Guy Bolton, Jean Holloway, and Fred Finklehoffe had to come up with an analogous situation that wouldn't run afoul of the censors. Even more importantly there were the sensibilities of audiences to consider. While moviegoers enjoyed seeing a Franklin Pangborn doing his pansy bit in small doses, you couldn't build an entire film around a homosexual—that would be a crime against the nature of the box office.

So the writers approached things the only way they could. The Larry Hart of *Words and Music* falls hard. For a woman. The fictitious Peggy McNeil is a struggling actress played by Betty Garrett. The two pal around for a while but then, for unspecified reasons and all evidence to the contrary, she tells him she's not in love with him. In the normal course of things, a fella would have laid low for a little bit, licked his wounds, and then found someone new. But not our Larry Hart. He spends the rest of the film obsessed with his unattainable *amorosa*. While Richard Rodgers marries an angel, Larry Hart sulks. He throws huge but hollow Hollywood parties. He has a drunken scene. He tries to eradicate the memory of Betty Garrett by spending time with cheap women. (Or as Drake's Richard Rodgers enunciates it, "Confused and dispirited, among strange people in strange places, he was just a lost guy.")

Despite all this despair, Rooney is still zipping around like a whirling dervish, all manic energy with only the occasional slightly pained expression on his face. The movie does not bother delving into their breakup or the fact that Rodgers had already teamed up with Oscar Hammerstein II before Hart died. But it does show the hospitalized Hart determined to attend a revival of one of his early hits, *A Connecticut Yankee*, and if much of what has come before this was ridiculous, now we're truly into the theater of the absurd. After making it to the show he goes back outside in the rain, stumbles, collapses, and dies, looking for all the world

Does the man on the left look full of self-loathing to you? As lyricist Lorenz Hart, Mickey Rooney has fun joining in an old-fashioned sing-a-long with Tom Drake, Betty Garrett, and Janet Leigh.

as if he's doing a parody of James Cagney's death scene in *The Roaring Twenties*; while Cagney died on church steps, Hart expires outside the shoe store where he had bought those mirth-provoking elevator lifts.

Then there's the movie's coda after Hart has died and different performers appear in a memorial service paying him tribute in song. One of the participants is Perry Como. There's ostensibly nothing odd about that—except that we've seen Como throughout the film, playing a fictional character, a friend of the composers named Eddie Anders. Now he's presenting himself as Perry Como. It's positively postmodernistic.

Mickey Rooney is a versatile performer, but certain emotions are outside of his range: he's too much an optimistic, upbeat presence to convey the anguish, doubt, and self-laceration that were so much a part of Lorenz Hart. It's also difficult to accept Rooney dealing with any problems more serious than Andy Hardy's having to decide whether to take Polly Benedict or the new girl in town to the prom. Rooney wrote in his autobiography that *Words and Music* was "a terrible turkey, and I knew it as soon as I saw the shooting script." Richard Rodgers would later say, "The only good thing about that picture was that they had Janet Leigh play my wife. And I found *that* highly acceptable."

At the helm of *Words and Music* was the prolific but dreary Norman Taurog, who would wind down his career directing some of Elvis's last and least movies (*Speedway* and *Live a Little, Love a Little*), as well as the Frankie Avalon vehicles *Sergeant Deadhead* and *Dr. Goldfoot and the Bikini Machine*. Improbable but true: Despite featuring appearances by Judy Garland, Gene Kelly, Lena Horne, and Mel Torme, *Words and Music* is even sorrier than that quartet of films.

John Wayne

The Conqueror (1954; released 1956)

"Mongol Cowboy"

Every once in a while, a casting choice can seem not merely illogical but downright insane: what in the world could have gone on at the meetings in which such and such an actor was suggested, enthused about, and approved. John Wayne as Genghis Kahn?

Howard Hughe's studio publicists wanted you to believe that Wayne's participation in *The Conqueror* occurred just so:

> A champion like Wayne can and must choose his pictures carefully, and that's just what he did with *The Conqueror*. Dropping by producer-director Dick Powell's office to discuss an entirely different story, Wayne spied *The Conqueror* script on Dick's desk and asked what it was. When Powell had sketched the theme briefly Wayne asked to borrow the script overnight, called early the next morning to say: "Let's do *this* one—it's great!" With the screen's top star set, Powell had little trouble in getting a front office O.K. for the biggest budget in RKO history.

The truth, of course, was somewhat more involved. Dick Powell had been counting on borrowing Marlon Brando from 20th Century–Fox to star in his picture. Brando was going to be otherwise engaged, however, playing a militant from a different time and place—Napoleon Bonaparte in *Desiree*—meaning *The Conqueror* would have to do without the cinema's current golden boy. It so happened that John Wayne had signed a two-picture deal with RKO and still owed the studio a film. Faced with an expensive project with no leading man, the studio called in its chits. This was clearly a good news/bad news situation. On the positive side,

How not to look like Genghis Khan.

even though Brando would have brought more prestige, Wayne was, nevertheless, a bigger box-office draw in 1954 (on that year's exhibitors' poll, Wayne was voted number-one star in the country, Brando ten). The downside was the wildly different styles and capabilities of the two actors. Screenwriter Oscar Millard, enthused at the prospect of having his lines spoken by Brando, had already completed his script. Brando had excelled at the Elizabethan English of *Julius Caesar*, so the writer set out to create his very own Millard-ian poetry for the actor. Or, as he explained it, "Carried away, I decided to write the screenplay in stylized, slightly archaic English." Boy, was he surprised to learn that it would be John Wayne who would be saying such lines as "She is a woman, much woman. Should her perfidy be less than other women?"

It used to be fashionable to deride John Wayne as a one-dimensional actor, but that's now conceded to have been a facile evaluation. He frequently did outstanding work, especially in the films he made for John Ford. Wayne's elegiac performance as a senescent calvary officer in *She Wore a Yellow Ribbon* holds its own as one of the half-dozen or so most beautiful film performances by any actor. But it *is* true that the actor could frequently be lazy and simply play John Wayne on screen. *The Conqueror* was one of those times. Which was unfortunate since there was quite a gulf between the Mongolian warrior and the mythic American that John Wayne had come to represent.

The Conqueror is peculiar. It opens with Genghis Khan (actually, throughout the movie his name is Temujin—he's given his more famous handle at the end of the picture) encountering Bortai (Susan Hayward), the red-tressed daughter of a Tartar chief on her way to be married to the head of the Merkits. He decides that she is a bit of all right (or letting him speak for himself, "I feel this Tartar woman is for me. My blood says take her.") Never mind that her dad killed his dad, Temujin and his horde swoop down and kidnap her from her betrothed. The Mongols handily defeat the Merkits, and the first thing Temujin does is humiliatingly rip off Bortai's dress in front of his army, handing it to the vanquished fiancé as a souvenir.

What then follows is an unsettling exhibition of sexual harassment as he puts the moves on her and she alternately fends off his advances and stews. Bortai is a spitfire, hurling insults at her captor ("Is Temujin so wanting for a woman that he will quench his fire with ice?")—and you quickly realize that scripter Millard, with his visions of Brando, did have Shakespeare on the brain, for the movie plays like a cheesy reworking of *The Taming of the Shrew*. After Bortai tries to slice off Temujin's head, he rhapsodizes, "Yer beautiful in yer wrath."

Eventually she realizes she's in love with the man who assaulted her and, plotwise, *The Conqueror* then becomes a fairly typical sword-and-sand adventure. Temujin gets to work on consummating his dream of eradicating the Tartars and becoming grand poobah of all the Mongol tribes. He's ultimately successful, although only after a lot of blood-letting and back-stabbing intrigue, as well as familial arguments, misunderstandings, and recriminations. By the fade-out, he is finally declared to be Genghis Khan, which translates into "the perfect warrior," and settles into happily ever after with his Tartar wife.

Watching *The Conqueror*, you can't decide what's goofier, the way Wayne sounds speaking his lines or the way he looks, dressed to the nines in twelfth-century Mongolian splendor. He sports a Fu Manchu moustache and a toupee that calls to mind Moe Howard; his eyes are taped to give him a slight Asian flavor; and his helmet is not unlike that worn by Kaiser Wilhelm, but accessorized with a patch of fur. This look does not become him. Clearly uncomfortable—and reportedly sauced much of the time—Wayne sounds as if he's reading his lines phonetically; he must have had some struggle getting to the point where he could spout off such non-household names as "Jumuga," "Kumlek," and "Targutai." He is so unsteady in the role that ultimately he comes across like an amateur John Wayne impersonator wearing a funny costume. In fairness to Wayne, Marlon Brando would have been just as helpless when faced with the challenge of expressing such sentiments as "I am bereft of spit," and "You didn't suckle me to be slain by Tartars, my mother, but to destroy them." (Wayne's crabby mom was Agnes Moorehead—only six months older than he.) His most exquisite moment occurs when, the Mongol cause looking bad, Temujin heads to the top of a mountain and starts talking—with the help of an echo machine—to the "eternal skies" and the "spirits of Heaven." "Send me men! Men!" he clamors and, griping that, "I am beset by weaklings and traitors, and victory is slipping from my grasp," he beseeches, "Let not treachery prevail!" They comply.

Wayne said he saw the movie pretty much as a Western. "The way the screenplay read, it is a cowboy picture and that is how I am going to play Genghis Khan. I see him as a gunfighter." If it had been set in the Badlands instead of the Gobi desert, if the characters had names like Tex and the Kid and not Wang Khan, and if the men wore chaps rather than armor, *The Conqueror* would probably have passed unnoticed as just another John Wayne Western.

THE RACE CARD

Ethnic impersonations that might well have set race relations back decades. Who needs verisimilitude when you can have a movie star?

Glenn Ford, Paul Ford, and Eddie Albert are all startled by something, but it's Marlon Brando as a stereotypical inscrutable Asian that will have the audience disconcerted.

Marlon Brando

The Teahouse of the August Moon (1956)

"Dis-Oriented"

Dealing playfully with the American occupational forces in postwar Okinawa, John Patrick's play *The Teahouse of the August Moon* was spectacularly successful when it premiered in 1953, winning the Pulitzer, Tony, and New York Drama Critics awards and running for two and a half years. Yet it is rarely revived. No wonder: maybe back then people didn't know any better, but today its humorous theme of Westerners finding themselves outsmarted by wily Asians would be deemed offensive by everyone except perhaps Pat Buchanan enthusiasts. Although it was written with all the best liberal humanistic intentions, *Teahouse* would certainly not be considered politically correct by today's standards.

How strange, then, to find front and center in the film version Marlon Brando, a man who was P.C. before P.C. was cool. Moreover, he's the most objectionable thing in the movie. Brando had let MGM know he was interested in the role of Sakini, a mischievous Okinawa native, as soon as he heard *Teahouse* was going to be turned into a movie. Gentle satire it might have been, but Brando thought *Teahouse* was really sticking it to the arrogant American impulse to impose this country's attitudes and traditions on the rest of the world. In addition, having proven adept at old-timey English in *Julius Caesar*, he was now looking to try his hand at a different language altogether—Japanese—combined with an Asian version of pidgin-English. Brando learned Japanese by rote, and to the untrained ear he sounded authentic even though he didn't understand what he was saying. The actor said that more difficult than learning Japanese was trying to forget English and then relearn it differently. He honed his version of broken English by listening to Japanese natives speaking it.

Even Brando had his limitations, and they are evident in *Teahouse*: from time to time, he fails to sustain his accent and returns to his prototypical Method mumbling and proletarian patois. Occasionally he sounds like he is *On the Waterfront*'s Terry Malloy, now hiding from union boss Lee J. Cobb, not on the rooftops of Hoboken but in an Asian village. Brilliant actor he may be, yet here Brando is not much different from any of those who have played Charlie Chan. Despite his intense preparation, ultimately he does nothing unusual with the role: in hackneyed fashion, his *l*'s become *r*'s and vice versa so, for instance, in wishing someone felicitations, he says, "Good ruck." He even throws in an "Ah, so" or two.

Brando's character is the local translator for army captain Glenn Ford, who has been assigned to teach the citizens of a small Okinawese town about democracy while building them a new school. But those humorously inscrutable Orientals prefer a teahouse, a symbol of their own culture, to a structure in which their children would be indoctrinated with Western values, and they use all their considerable cunning on Ford to get their way. The captain's blowhard commanding officer (Paul Ford) is appalled at his failure to follow through on his orders, and all sorts of conventional complications ensue. Everything turns out A-OK, with lessons learned regarding brotherhood and Our Common Humanity. Highly praised at the time, and one of the top-grossing films of 1956, *The Teahouse of the August Moon* today plays as a standard military farce, occasionally funny but more often too frantic for its own good. Asked by Colonel Paul Ford, "Where's your get up and go?" Brando, of course, replies, "Guess get up and go went, boss."

Brando used rubber lids over his tear ducts to look sloe-eyed, went on a crash diet so that his cheekbones would be highlighted, slapped on a black wig, and attached protruding fake teeth for a clichéd overbite. Nothing could be done about his very Caucasian Roman nose short of rhinoplasty. He hunches over, both to downplay his size and to try to convey servility, constantly smiles (as stereotyped Asians do all of the time), juts out his chin, gesticulates expansively, and moves in a busy, scuttling gait. In short, he expended a lot of energy. For all that, one never loses sight that this is American movie star Marlon Brando wearing yellow greasepaint. Four decades after aggressively going after the part, Brando admitted in his memoirs, "I was badly miscast in *The Teahouse of the August Moon*."

Chuck Connors

Geronimo (1962)

"Wooden Indian"

The casting of Chuck Connors as Geronimo demonstrates the at-one-time-common Hollywood thinking that you could throw a long, straight black wig on anyone and have an instant Indian. With his absurdly angular features and bright blue eyes, Connors was nobody's idea of a Native American, except, apparently, producer-director Arnold Laven. Connors had become a star in the television series *The Rifleman*, and Laven seems to have figured that a Western's a Western. Cowboy, Indian—what's the difference?

Geronimo is a low-budget second feature, an unadorned account of a few dozen Apaches who declare war on the United States after the land they've cultivated on their reservation is confiscated. About the only positive thing to say about the movie is that it comes down on the side of the angels (although by 1962 being pro–Native American was not exactly controversial).

Call him a minimalist actor or simply call him wooden, but Connors is incapable of communicating any sense of Geronimo's passion; he lacks the magnetism that would make you believe that a band of men would happily follow him into battle despite overwhelming odds. One also feels that the Apaches would be less than eager to put their trust in a leader who has the piercing azure eyes of the White Man. Connors does little more than stare impassively as he stews over the deceitful ways of his vanquisher, and his dialogue is recited with a decided lack of emotion. (His innate inexpressiveness marks Chuck Connors as the least likely native of Brooklyn imaginable.) It would take an actor with considerably more panache than Connors to make a line like "I've decided I need a

Taking a respite from playing a gunslinger on TV's *The Rifleman*, Chuck Connors merely looks like a cowboy in a fright wig. Cavalry officer Pat Conway is speaking with forked tongue, so he'll get his.

woman" sound anything other than ludicrous. *Films and Filming* laughed that Connors "is far from convincing and he sounds more like a cowboy Tarzan than a 'noble savage.' "

A rumor dogged Chuck Connors throughout his career. Everyone was aware that he played, briefly and not very well, Major League baseball for the Brooklyn Dodgers and Chicago Cubs. But those well-versed in celebrity gossip snickered that he had started in show biz by strutting his stuff to gay audiences in the era's equivalent of porno movies. Referred to as "physique"—or to make them sound wholesome, "nature"—films, these shorts featured actors who didn't actually engage in any physical activities other than, say, tossing a beach ball. But whatever they did, they did in the nude. Now, I've never seen any proof that Connor's theatrical origins can be traced to this particular form of entertainment. It must be said, however, that in *Geronimo* he performs with the sort of torpor you'd associate with someone who's exhausted from the physical rigors of making dirty movies.

Blythe Danner and Judith Ivey

Brighton Beach Memoirs (1986)

"Gentile on My Mind"

Blythe Danner has long worked her magic on theatergoers, so it does seem unfair that moviegoers have been given so few opportunities to be entranced by her. In 1986, the welcomed news that Danner was being cast in a lead role in a major studio release, was, however, tempered by irony: talented as she is, she was simply ill suited for the film version of Neil Simon's *Brighton Beach Memoirs*. Here was a quintessential WASP portraying a quintessential Jewish mother. Another Broadway star, Judith Ivey from El Paso, Texas, got the call to play Danner's sister. Flaxen-haired and fair-skinned, the two actresses could easily pass as members of the same family, just not *this* family. Sipping lemonade on a veranda in North Carolina or hobknobbing at a Fairfield County cocktail party, Danner and Ivey would have made perfect sense together. But in working-class Brooklyn of the thirties, they are alien presences.

Onstage, *Brighton Beach Memoirs* was said to have signaled the arrival of a new, mature Neil Simon. Some maturity. Drawing upon his own adolescent experiences, Simon wrote a smarmy comedy preoccupied with a teenage boy's obsession with masturbation and breasts; its second-act revelations of "ugly truths" about long-held resentments played like Arthur Miller Lite. (Critic Stanley Kauffman wrote, "On stage we were all aware that this was *Neil Simon*'s autobiography and we were meant to be especially appreciative that a hugely successful Broadway figure was disclosing his past.") The members of the New York Drama Critics Circle were appropriately grateful: they gave it the award for Best Play of the Year.

When *Brighton Beach Memoirs* was turned into a movie, the casting of Danner as a *yiddische mama* and Ivey as Aunt Blanche raised more

A couple of shiksahs with their Jewish relatives. (Museum of Modern Art/Film Stills Archives)

than a few eyebrows. It's saying a lot, then, that the participation of the two actresses is far from the worst thing about the film. Gene Saks may have won a Tony for directing *Brighton Beach Memoirs* on the stage, but as a filmmaker he's always had an uncanny knack for depleting any vitality from the material he's been handed. Directing his first movie since *Mame*, Saks gives the film even less resonance than he did the original play. Whenever he adapts his own plays into films, Neil Simon shows a respect for his original words that borders on the slavish. His inelegant dialogue remains intact, forever preserved. (Two examples of the famous Simon wit—Older Brother to Younger: "The whole world whacks off." Younger Brother to Older: "You smell up the bathroom. When I go in there I have to puke.") *Brighton Beach Memoirs* is two hours of wisecracks without a single laugh. Whining incessantly as the young Neil Simon counterpart, the grating Jonathan Silverman is a bargain-basement knockoff of Matthew Broderick, whose sly flippancy gave the stage production what little value it had. Clearly, even if the two female leads had been ideally cast, this movie wasn't going to amount to anything much. But still . . .

Danner's Mama Kate is in no way an original dramatic creature. How many times have we seen this loud-but-loving, know-it-all Jewish mother, and from the moment she first appears we know that underneath a harsh exterior strongly beats a heart of gold. Ivey is equally stereotyped as a young widow with two daughters, a sickly constitution, and a benignly anxious outlook on life. Both actresses have kept their usual hair shades; true, there are blond Jewish women, but it is a little jarring to have such clichéd behavior and stock emotions coming from two women so atypical in appearance.

Russian Jews seem to be a most exotic species to Danner and Ivey. The two of them are adrift in their attempt to nail down the vocal rhythms of their characters and then communicate some sense of the lower-middle-class immigrant experience beyond those dubious accents. David Denby of *New York* conceded that, "the talented Gentile ladies try hard," but added that "what Blythe Danner and Judith Ivey don't realize is that Jewish-American women of the 1930s did not speak with rising inflections (Danner) or a panicked drone (Ivey) in every single sentence—there was considerable variety."

Neil Simon does not exactly write in a naturalistic vein. His characters don't have conversations; they're forever engaged in verbal one-upmanship, determined to outdo each other with quips, putdowns, and observations. The movie's artificiality makes it harder to overlook that it's that nice shiksa Blythe Danner and Judith Ivey, who always does so well in those Southern roles, who are trying to pass for Jewish. You get the feeling that if someone in this household came down with a cold, Danner wouldn't serve chicken soup but a tray of hors d'oeuvres and Welsh rarebit on toast points. And, by the way, why is Danner's character named Kate? Other than some variation on Maureen or Colleen, it would be hard to think of a name that more immediately conjures up the image of a bonny Irish lass. Which is what Blythe Danner is.

John Garfield, Hedy Lamarr, Frank Morgan, and Spencer Tracy

Tortilla Flat (1942)

"Mexican Standoff"

During the so-called Golden Age of Movies, Hollywood couldn't have cared less about authenticity when it came to ethnic groups other than WASPs and the Irish. *Tortilla Flat* can serve as the prosecution's exhibit number one.

The picaresque John Steinbeck book on which the film was based consists of vignettes about Mexican Americans living outside of Monterey, California. The *paisanos* of *Tortilla Flat* offered Steinbeck's readers a chance to go slumming with a sentimental bunch who would have been much too earthy to associate with in real life. There is virtually no plot in the book; the movie has the barest minimum: Danny (John Garfield) inherits two houses and a watch from his grandfather. His pal, Pilon (Spencer Tracy), spends most of the film using reverse psychology to induce him to barter away his possessions for enough wine and food to keep their whole gang happy. Danny becomes infatuated with Dolores (Hedy Lamarr), a no-nonsense Portuguese woman, and Pilon schemes to undermine their burgeoning relationship, cognizant that her stabilizing influence will put end to his domination of Danny.

There is much drinking of wine, good-natured needling, and singing of bawdy songs. But you'd never think these demi-Rabelaisian acts are being engaged in by anyone of Mexican descent. Most of the cast members don't even take a stab at accents—the only indications of the characters' ethnicity are their names and the sombreros situated on various heads.

John Garfield may look reasonably Mexican, but wait until he opens his mouth. Spencer Tracy is just Spencer Tracy wearing a funny hat.

A lot of people con-sider Spencer Tracy the best screen actor ever. No evidence of that here. He makes Pilon a likable rogue, but the extent of his playing Latino is to speak at a clipped pace while expressing himself with excessive formality—saying, for example, "in which to catch it," rather than "to catch it in"—as Latinos a-lways seem to do in the movies. If Tracy entertained ideas of speaking with a Mexican timbre, such thoughts absconded before filming began.

John Garfield *does* speak with an accent, but it's the sound of his New York City roots. When he calls Dolores "Sweets" the first time he meets her, he evokes the image of a wolf standing on the corner of Broadway and 42nd Street. Garfield is, as always, supremely charismatic, and his fusing of nonchalant confidence and—any time Danny goes up against Pilon or Dolores—abrupt perturbation makes for a memorable character. If only the "Flat" in the title had been short for Flatbush, he would have been perfect.

You could watch *Tortilla Flat* a dozen times and still not have a clue about what Hedy Lamarr is up to. In each scene, the Viennese-born

Pigtails cannot turn an Austrian beauty into a Portuguese-American working girl.

actress tries out a new elocution. Playing a young woman who works in a canning factory, she sounds in one scene like a heart-of-gold hash slinger, in the next, she's the Empress of Austria. Now she apes Garfield's Rivington Street accent; later you'd swear she was a housewife from the American Midwest. Not until Sally Field's *Sybil* did an actress portray so many different characters in a single film. (Critic Manny Farber winced that "whenever Hedy Lamarr opens her mouth the wrong words with the wrong feeling invariably come out.") At the time a lot was made of the fact that glamourpuss Lamarr was dressing down. *Life* scooped, "For the first time in her career, Hedy depends on no glamorous clothes or background to enhance her charms. She wears no fake eyelashes, no makeup except a 10-cent lipstick and grease to darken her skin. Her costume cost only $3.95, and took only four minutes to slip into." If only they had taken the money they saved on wardrobe and shelled out for a diction coach.

Frank Morgan is also in the movie. One of the more esteemed actors of his time, he'll forever be known as the title character in *The Wizard of Oz*; in *Tortilla Flat*, Morgan is a gnarly old hermit, "the Pirate," who serves as the film's redemptive figure. Pilon hopes to bilk the Pirate out of the money he has been hoarding—how else can he afford more wine?—but it turns out the old boy is saving up for a gold candlestick to place before a statue of his patron, St. Francis of Assisi. Overhearing the Pirate discussing St. Francis with his beloved dogs, Pilon sees the errors of his way and vows to become a better, if less interesting, person. Morgan has a long, scraggly beard so he looks the part, but when he starts acting he falls back on his fluttery mannerisms and customary hemming-and-hawing speech patterns. He's a simple Mexican American, but he has you convinced he's still living in the Emerald City.

The Wizard of Oz goes slumming.

At the time of *Tortilla Flat*, John Steinbeck was firmly ensconced in the pantheon of American men of letters, and *The Grapes of Wrath* and *Of Mice and Men* had recently been made into movies revered by critics. With its unconvincing characterizations and strained whimsy, *Tortilla Flat* proved to be one of the more disappointing motion pictures of 1942. As the *New York World-Telegram* harrumphed, "it is dull, pretentious, heavy-handed, and phony, with its star-studded cast as much the blame as anyone, for seldom have I seen Spencer Tracy, John Garfield, and Frank Morgan so hokumish."

Alec Guinness

A Passage to India (1984)

"White Man's Burden"

A *Passage to India* was director David Lean's first movie in fourteen years. His adaptation of the E. M. Forster novel is visually impressive, unprofound, and entertaining in a stolid sort of way. In Lean's hands, the book went from a symbolism-flecked social comedy with dark overtones to a fairly straightforward tract about the English colonization of India. That it was greeted so warmly by reviewers in 1984 (and named Best Picture by the New York Film Critics) attests more to feelings of auld lang syne toward the director than to the quality of the film. At age seventy-six, Lean was still making movies the old-fashioned way—and that included casting a white British guy as an Indian wise man.

Lean's old friend and frequent star, Alec Guinness, is the Brahmin educator and philosopher Professor Godbole. Guinness's fussy comic style and penchant for digging into his makeup box to make himself unrecognizable dates back to 1949's *Kind Hearts and Coronets*, in which he played eight different murder victims. But in *A Passage to India*, he calls to mind the actor who was his immediate successor as the eccentric star of droll little British comedies that played art houses in the States. Though it's unlikely that he intended it, Sir Alec's performance as Professor Godbole serves as an homage to Peter Sellers.

In Blake Edwards's *The Party*, Sellers played a sweet-natured movie star from India who obliviously—and hilariously—lays waste to a Hollywood soiree. In keeping with the playfully rambunctious tone of the movie, Sellers's overemphatic accent is intentionally absurd. Despite the loftiness that permeates *A Passage to India*, Alec Guinness sounds very much like Sellers. If you've seen *The Party*, Guinness's performance will inevitably put you in mind of such images as Peter Sellers desperately

searching the house for an unoc-
cupied bathroom and then causing the toilet to overflow. You
might well find yourself chuck-
ling to yourself in the midst of
such serious moments in *A Passage to India* as Mrs. Moore's
death scene or the arrest of Dr.
Aziz for attempted rape.

Even for people who haven't
viewed *The Party*—or don't have
Arte Johnson's Eastern mystic on
Laugh-In as a point of reference—Guinness is still a jarring
presence in *A Passage to India*
because he is so out of sync with
his fellow actors. Amidst the
subtle and impressively under-

Peek-a-boo! Alec Guinness would have
startled anyone who was expecting even a
remotely accurate portrayal of an Indian
intellectual.

stated performances of Judy Davis, Victor Banerjee, Peggy Ashcroft, and
James Fox, Sir Alec appears to be in his own movie. He turns Godbole
into a physically comic figure. Shoulders stooped, Guinness doesn't walk,
he waddles. He's also busy doing all sorts of odd things with his face: bug-
ging out his glassy eyes, raising his eyebrows, gumming his lips. None of
the Indian actors in *A Passage to India* behave in this manner. The med-
itative character of Godbole functions in the story as a metaphor for the
proposition that the customs and idiosyncrasies of one culture will
inevitably remain enigmatic to another. The aphorisms that Godbole is
constantly spouting are simpleminded on the surface but may or may not
be profound when you mull them over. In Guinness's exaggerated delivery, everything he says seems like a put-on: the actor has eliminated the
ambiguities of his character.

The performance transforms what should be a lightly off-centered,
whimsical character into a numskull. Guinness especially comes up short
compared to Calcutta-born Victor Banerjee, a star in his native country,
who, seemingly effortlessly, brings humor, quiet grandeur, and a great deal
of charm to Dr. Aziz, the cultured physician who is put on trial. It's to
the movie's benefit that Alec Guinness has only a handful of scenes, which
is a surprising thing to have to be saying about a certified Great Actor.

Katharine Hepburn

Dragon Seed (1944)
Song of Love (1947)

"Globe Trotter"

Dorothy Parker remarked that Katharine Hepburn ran the gamut of emotions from A to B. That was unfair. Hepburn almost always got to at least E. Wonderful in sophisticated comedies—running all the way to Z—and in roles that gave full rein to her independent streak, Hepburn had limitations as an actress that became all too apparent when she was miscast. In *Dragon Seed*, she was stuck on A as a Chinese peasant.

What is most sublime about Hepburn's Asian adventure is that she is playing an agrarian Chinese woman who speaks in the rarified accent of upper-crust Connecticut. "The Great Kate" did submit to the obligatory taping of her eyelids (with fish skin) for a dab of Oriental flavor, but she had apparently gotten it into her head that it was fine for her character, named Jade, to sound like Katharine Hepburn. A Bryn Mawr graduate tilling the land outside Nanking?

Hepburn's Asian makeup is too understated to offset the jarring effect of her patrician voice. She looks vaguely Eurasian; it's as if makeup artist Jack Dawn dawdled on the first day of production and Hepburn was called to the set with her makeup only half done. Most of the cast members are fitted with high cheekbones; Hepburn's are already very pronounced, so the prosthetics don't make a great deal of difference. (When it was announced that she would star in *Dragon Seed*, one jokester quipped, "Any similarity between Katharine Hepburn and Jade would doubtless be purely occidental.") None of the Caucasian cast members looks particularly Asian, and several of them (Hurd Hatfield, Agnes Moorehead) are so waxlike and unrealistic that they hardly seem human

Nanking by way of Bryn Mawr. Katharine Hepburn in *Dragon Seed*.

at all. Meanwhile, the children of the various couples are played by gen-uine Asian youngsters; not resembling their on-screen parents in the least, they give the impression of having been adopted.

A number of Jade's character traits are appropriate for Hepburn, but her nationality is not one of them. Jade is a saucy, strong-willed woman; she believes a wife should be more than a glorified servant who is so nice to have around the house only to bear offspring, and, a rarity among woman of her background, she also knows how to read. (MGM public-ity bragged that *Dragon Seed* "glorifies the modern Chinese girl.") These attributes are pure Hepburn, making Jade an Asian cousin of *Little Women*'s Jo, as well as Pamela Thistlethwaite, the eponymous character of what could be the generic Hepburn movie title, *A Woman Rebels*.

Based on a novel by Pearl S. Buck, *Dragon Seed* chronicles Japan's 1937 invasion of China and its disastrous impact on a close-knit farming family. Fiercely partisan in tone, the film, which studio executives thought of as "Mrs. Miniver Goes to China," presents a constrast between the simple dignity of the peace-loving Chinese and the unfettered brutality of the Japanese, referred to as "evil dwarfs." The barbarity of the conquer-ing forces arouses intense patriotism among the clan, and before long

Making like Clara Schumann, Hepburn hits the eighty-eights in *Song of Love*.

almost all of the family members are busying themselves with acts of resistance. The ne plus ultra incident in Jade's guerrilla activities is her slipping a vial of poison into the sauce at a banquet for upper-echelon Japanese officers. The sight of these evil dwarf bastards retching in agony before meeting eternal damnation must have been immensely satisfying to American audiences at the time.

Dragon Seed has its moments, especially in its relatively unflinching depiction of wartime atrocities. Even if what appears on-screen is only a pale approximation of what the Japanese were up to in China, it's remarkable to see rape so strongly suggested in a mid-forties MGM movie. Other images, such as the lynched bodies of resistance fighters blowing in the wind, a small child sitting in the snow next to the corpse of her mother, and starving people fighting over the carcass of a dog are still potent.

It's too bad, then, that the laudable aspects of *Dragon Seed* are undermined and overwhelmed by the ludicrous performances. In the same way that you can close your eyes whenever Katharine Hepburn is speaking and think she is still playing spoiled heiress Tracy Lord in *The Philadelphia Story*, Walter Huston, as family patriarch Ling Tan, sounds exactly like his

Midwestern industrialist in *Dodsworth* and George M. Cohan's father in *Yankee Doodle Dandy*. On a respite from his Maria Montez sword-and-sandal adventures, Turhan Bey—Austrian-born, of Turkish and Czech heritage—did not disguise his ripe continental tones; he should have been in a movie about anti-Nazi freedom fighters instead of going up against the Japanese. And Akim Tamiroff belongs on the Russian front. For sheer ridiculousness, however, the cast member who best matches Hepburn is Henry Travers. Two years before portraying Clarence the Angel in *It's a Wonderful Life*, the Irish native here plays a Chinese scholar. From the way Travers talks and carries himself, anyone seeing *Dragon Seed* today would swear Clarence was trying to persuade a Chinese peasant that if he hadn't been born the Great Wall would no longer be standing.

In *Song of Love*, Katharine Hepburn once again is an unconvincing citizen of another country. As in *Dragon Seed*, the actress does nothing to modify her voice, so she makes for an unusual-sounding German. This time, though, it isn't so much the nationality that's the problem, it's the character's disposition. Hepburn plays Clara Wieck, a young woman who is among the most highly renowned concert pianists in Europe. She falls in love with the up-and-coming composer Robert Schumann (Paul Henried) and—here's the unbelievable part—once she becomes Frau Schumann, she kisses off her career in order to raise their seven children and offer moral support for her husband (being a mercurial sort, he certainly needs it). Yes, Clara Schumann did this in actuality, but subjugating one's own aspirations is not something you can believe in Katharine Hepburn.

There have been numerous occasions when Hepburn has been totally believable playing a woman in love. But no matter how head-over-heels her characters may be, the actress's persona was established early on as someone who would be a coequal in any relationship. At one point in *Song of Love,* Schumann chides the housekeeper for not getting more work done: "Mrs. Schumann is an artist. She has no business bathing babies, scrubbing floors, making beds." To which Bertha responds, "What's an artist doing with all them children?" What indeed? There were any number of pleasant young actresses at MGM perfectly suited to taking care of the kids and telling her husband how grand he is. Not Katharine Hepburn, who was too strong and self-assertive for that kind of thing. (For a purported biography of a Great Composer, *Song of Love* spends an inordinate amount of time on obstreperous children and domestic drudgery.) Even when Clara makes a triumphal return engagement to the concert stage, it's only to pay off her not-yet-acclaimed husband's bills. And despite the entreaties of Germany's number one impresario, Mrs. Schumann makes it a one-night stand and heads back to domesticity. (In *Song of Love*'s silliest scene, Clara rushes through her last number in the concert because her youngest child is backstage impatiently waiting to be nursed.)

Nor can Hepburn making us believe she's living in the mid-nineteenth century. She has too much sly puckishness and subtle good humor in her to be Frau Schumann. The actress has excelled in period pieces, but only when her characters have gone against the conventions of the era: modern women ahead of their times. In *Song of Love*, Clara Schuman lets her rare talent wither away so she can stand by her man. Once Robert dies, Clara is free to marry Johannes Brahms (Robert Walker), a friend of the family who has long been in love with her. She declines, preferring instead to tackle the concert stage. You feel like cheering: freed from the tether of her dour husband, she's finally going to be her own woman and get the fame and glory due her. But no. The noble Mrs. Schumann is hitting the road to play music written by her husband, the better to propagate his majesty. You throw your hands up in exasperation.

Boris Karloff

Unconquered (1947)

"Forked Tongue"

Here's how Cecil B. DeMille's thinking went: Boris Karloff plays villains. Gyuasuta, chief of the Senecas, is a villain. Ergo, Boris Karloff would be ideal as Guyasuta, chief of the Senecas. The result: *Unconquered*, DeMille's impossibly hokey epic dealing with conflicts between Indians and settlers in pre-Revolutionary America, contains the most urbane savage brute imaginable, complete with a British accent.

Given titles like "King of the Monsters" and the "Titan of Terror," Karloff had a standing as the consummate sadist, madman, and all-around miscreant that stemmed largely from the very mellifluousness of his voice. That someone as much a gentleman as Karloff could implant a malignant brain in a healthy man (*The Man Who Lived Again*), cruelly govern over the inmates of an insane asylum (*Bedlan*), and kill the boy princes (*Tower of London*) meant that *anyone* was capable of committing unspeakable acts. Karloff—friends always referred to him as "dear Boris"—is no gentleman in *Unconquered*. He's a ruthless, bloodthirsty beast and a menace to white maidenhood. There were never any gradations of character in Cecil B. DeMille's world.

Although fourth-billed, Karloff has only three scenes in the film. His Senecas have joined forces with other tribes in an attempt to stem the expansion of British settlements across North America. To that end, Karloff's braves kidnap Paulette Goddard and tie her to a stake. Chief Boris watches approvingly as she writhes in agony while being tickled with eagle feathers.

Frontiersman Gary Cooper is nuts about Paulette, a former indentured servant he earlier had bought and set free, and he's heard about

He's supposedly the fiercest Indian in the colonies, but Boris Karloff is more doleful than threatening.

"what they do to white women." But they'll do no such thing to Paulette, not if he has anything to say about it. The Indian scout and the Indian chief have enjoyed a social relationship over the years, so Karloff lets himself get talked into a deal: if Cooper can outdo the Senecas' medicine man in the magic department, Karloff will forego immolating Paulette. For his prestidigitation, Cooper employs one of those newfangled compasses, and Karloff is astounded when the arrow points where Cooper orders it to. By the time Chief Boris and his doctor figure out they've been snookered, Gary and Paulette have ducked out and are paddling away in a canoe. And about to go over a waterfall.

Boris Karloff's first screen appearance was as an Indian in *The Last of the Mohicans* in 1920. But that, of course, was a silent movie. Although *Unconquered* lists a credit for "Indian Language Advisor" (Iron Eyes Cody), Karloff mainly speaks in broken English. The contrast between the actor's cultured tones and the goobleygood he's mouthing is the comic highlight of this campy film. Making things even more irresistible, Karloff speaks with his customary slight lisp. Despite his festive Native American finery, the actor looks fairly glum as Guyasuta, and is devoid of the malicious glee he usually displays. (He was having serious problems with his back at the time and had to wear a heavy brace. Maybe that explains it.) Sad-eyed and frowning, his face surrounded by a long black wig, Karloff looks less like a proud warrior than a woebegone cocker spaniel.

Unconquered isn't as much fun when Karloff's not around. Still, the movie contains enough inane speeches ("I don't know what the good Lord was about when he made a female out of a perfectly good rib"; "You haven't blood in your veins, You've gun powder!"), hoary plot contrivances (and DeMille, natch, works in one of his trademark bathtub scenes), half-assed action sequences, and staggeringly bad performances to hold your interest in a perverse way. A huge crowd-pleaser back in 1947, *Unconquered* is stupid in the way that only a Cecil B. DeMille movie can be.

Donna Reed

The Far Horizons (1955)

"The Squaw Next Door"

What Donna Reed exuded on-screen was a warmheartedness and an undefinable "niceness"; a columnist for the *Los Angeles Daily News* even referred to her as "Nice Nellie." Hollywood generally gave credence to a dichotomous madonna/whore view of women, labeling actresses as either virgins or vamps, so Reed found herself pigeonholed in parts that glorified wholesome young ladies. Of all the actresses who played within this niche, she was one of the most appealing, for she possessed an intelligence and resolve that kept her performances grounded and prevented her from ever being either cloying or bland. Would Jimmy Stewart have seemed to have so much to live for if some other actress had played his wife in *It's a Wonderful Life*?

Accomplished as she was in these parts, Reed was always on the lookout for change-of-pace assignments that would give her acting chops a workout. "You know the type," she once said. "Shrewish, mean, disagreeable, but with just a thread of understandability, so the hate doesn't go too deep." Although her Oscar-winning performance as a prostitute in *From Here to Eternity* was affecting, she still seemed like the most ladylike hooker in history. It was that darned old all-American niceness again.

If you want to be literal about it, nothing could be more quintessentially all-American than a Native American, and in *The Far Horizons*, Donna Reed was cast as Sacajawea, the Shoshone Indian who guided the Lewis and Clark expedition. What emerged was an odd hybrid of two condescending stereotypes: the noble savage and the middle-class girl-next-door. In a completely fabricated narrative, Fred MacMurray's Lewis

Donna Reed makes Sacajawea look like the girl
from the teepee next door.

and Charlton Heston's Clark are onetime friends who have a falling out over women. First, Clark steals Lewis's girlfriend, upper-crust Washingtonian Barbara Hale. Then on the expedition Clark forgets about the girl he left behind and pitches woo to Sacajawea, which Lewis doesn't like at all.

Historians tell us that none of this actually happened and that, in fact, Sacajawea had a husband—a French-Canadian trader named Charboneau—who also tagged along on the trek. But where's the drama there? So while screenwriters Edmund North and Winston Miller included this Charboneau, they transformed him from a spouse to a louse, making him a treacherous rapscallion with designs on our heroine. While Lewis and Clark act peevishly toward each other, Reed's Shoshone goes about her business in leading them not just through the territory covered by the Louisiana Purchase territory, but all the way to the Pacific, which she quaintly refers to in Indian-speak as "the big salt water."

Clark and Sacajawea make plans to wed, and back in Washington he proudly shows her off to President Thomas Jefferson. But she also meets up with Barbara Hale's socialite. When Sacajawea asks her, "The wife of a white man, what does she do?" this woman of 1806 sounds just like a 1950's housewife: "She runs her husband's home. Entertains his friends. Tries to make him happy and successful and proud of being married to her." No wonder Sacajawea gets the hell out of there and rushes back to her own people.

Let's be honest. The real reason for this turn of events is that a run-of-the-mill Hollywood adventure movie from the mid-fifties was not about to sanction miscegenation, even when the non-Caucasian involved was Donna Reed. The movie downplays her ethnic heritage anyway: Clark claims that Sacajawea is too hard a name to pronounce, so throughout the film he calls her "Janie," as if to make the love affair more palatable for Eisenhower-era audiences.

As Sacajawea, Donna Reed is awfully pleasant, but not for a minute does she seem like a Native American. There are some scenes when she is side by side with actual female Indian extras who have high cheekbones, flat noses, and thick lips. You can't help but notice that Reed (born Donna Mullenger) doesn't possess these features. (The *Hollywood Reporter* declared that she "makes the most beautiful redskin the screen has offered.") Reed was given dark makeup, almost of the minstrel show variety, and bags under her eyes, but she still seems like a very nice Girl Scout leader who's participating in her troop's Thanksgiving pageant. Faced with the challenge of portraying a woman living off the land at the beginning of the nineteenth century, Reed speaks in a slow, measured meter. She was trying to make Sacajawea as dignified as possible. Deeply affected by the role, the actress campaigned to have Sacajawea elected into the Hall of Fame of Great Americans: "She's quite a gal and deserves to be in that special niche for great Americans at N.Y.U." Reed's efforts were unsuccessful.

Since the 1970s, actresses have justifiably complained that there are few good parts for women in the movies anymore, not like in the old days. It is startling to hear the pronouncement Donna Reed made *in the mid-1950s* about the state of things for movie actresses: "All the best roles today are written for men. Writers seem to have lost their interest in women. It's very difficult to find a part with all the elements in it." That is why she starred in but five more movies after *The Far Horizons* before switching over to television as a housewife and mother in her self-titled sitcom. Although not a world-beater in the laugh department, it lasted for nine years. *The Donna Reed Show* had one overriding appeal: its star was so very nice.

Edward G. Robinson

Our Vines Have Tender Grapes (1945)

"Norwegian Wood"

I used to believe that Edward G. Robinson could play anything. Having seen *Our Vines Have Tender Grapes*, I now believe that Edward G. Robinson could play anything except for a warmhearted, immigrant farmer from Norway. Perpetuated by generations of comic impressionists, the image of Robinson that immediately springs to mind is, of course, that of the pugnacious, cigar-chomping, staccato-speaking gangster, *see?* But over his fifty-year career, he played a wide spectrum of personalities, ranging from the dogged insurance investigator of *Double Indemnity* (steely but avuncular) to the chap who found a cure for syphilis in *Dr. Ehrlich's Magic Bullet* (dignified, scientific, and German) to a henpecked man getting suckered in by a femme fatale in *Scarlet Street* (vulnerable and pitiful). He was also an impeccable self-parodist, excelling in several comedies that kidded his tough-guy image. But this great actor was stymied by the phony-baloney sentimentality of *Our Vines Have Tender Grapes*.

A look at a Wisconsin farming community over the course of a year, *Our Vines Have Tender Grapes* is one of several films made during World War II about rural and small-town America and intended to emphasize what we were fighting for. (*The Human Comedy* with Mickey Rooney as a buttinsky Western Union boy was the most successful representative of this subgenre.) *Our Vines Have Tender Grapes* is chock-full of elements dear to the heart of MGM head Louis B. Mayer: family, patriotism, churchgoing, aggressively cute youngsters. (Ironically, this cloying piece of Americana was the last film written by Dalton Trumbo before he was blacklisted as a Communist.)

In *Our Vines Have Tender Grapes*, Edward G. Robinson had a whole
series of obstacles thrown at him: he had to come across as Norwegian,
deal with the scene-stealing of *two* kid actors—Margaret O'Brien and
Butch Jenkins—and try to seem interested in such activities as looking at
a cow. (Museum Modern Art/Film Stills Archives)

Our Vines Have Tender Grapes consists primarily of Robinson—husband to Agnes Moorehead and (rather old) father of Margaret O'Brien—
being sapient and reassuring to all those around him. He doles out
profundities like, "It's good to be happy." O'Brien emotes in her not-
unappealing grave manner and teeters on the verge of tears a lot; Moorehead frets a lot; and Butch Jenkins, as O'Brien's five-year-old cousin and
best playmate, says "shucks" a lot. This is a film in which the dramatic
highlight is Robinson's taking away Margaret's roller skates for being
mean to Butch. Another big scene: Margaret and Butch go for a boat ride
in a bathtub. Although the populace of Fuller Junction (a name suspi-
ciously redolent of Thornton Wilder's Grover's Corners) are undoubtedly
"good people," they're not a terribly interesting bunch, and you're most
likely to feel like newcomer schoolteacher Frances Gifford, sentenced to
a year in Fuller Junction as part of receiving her Ph.D. in education, who
(initially) can't wait to get out of there. Her analysis of local newspaper
editor James Craig's proposal of marriage is, "I don't want to hurt your

feelings but that's like saying 'I want to put you in jail. I want you to asso-ciate with dull, dreary people for all the rest of your life. I want to deny you all the opportunities of a civilized world.' "

A sophisticated, erudite man, Edward G. Robinson would undoubt-edly have died a slow death had he been stuck in Fuller Junction. When you hear him say, "Guess every man kind of figures way down in his heart, the one thing he really wants is a new barn," you immediately react, "No, he doesn't! Not any man that I know," and you can forgive Robinson his lack of conviction. (Old-timer Morris Carnovsky gets a spanking new barn at the beginning of the picture. When he acknowledges that he's put his entire fifty years' worth of life savings into the structure, it's your tip-off that the thing is going to burn down before the film is over. An hour later, it's gone.) Robinson's other most flagrantly atypical line is "I just killed twenty-one purebred Jerseys. A man can't sleep on that." (I could.)

Robinson doesn't make a believable farmer—he wasn't cut out to wear overalls—and he's an even less credible Norwegian. While most of the supporting players trot out approximations of heavy Norwegian accents, Robinson throws in a "yah" once or twice and lets it go at that. He also makes for an unusually dark Scandinavian. Going up against two kid actors, Robinson doesn't try to compete with them, and his under-playing results in an uncharacteristically listless performance. That lethargy was at least partially an acting choice for, in an attempt to impart the toll inflicted by the hard realities of agrarian life, the actor's move-ments are determinedly heavy and measured. Seeing a dynamic actor like Robinson in slow motion and acting at less than full strength feels like a gyp. But then none of the other performances rings true either. And the movie itself is hooey, self-consciously low-keyed and purposefully filled with "little moments." As a slice of life, it's as fake as all the painted backgrounds and obvious studio sets they're trying to palm off as verdant Wisconsin farmland.

Our Vines Have Tender Grapes—despite the title there's not a vine-yard in sight—was originally slated to be a Wallace Beery vehicle. The bumptious Beery wouldn't have been any more Norwegian than Robin-son, but he would have had one advantage over the far superior actor who replaced him: Beery registered rural. Unlike Robinson, he wouldn't have made you do a double-take when you saw him milking a cow.

GENERATION GAP

Actors who refused to age gracefully on-screen, and one who was in too much of a hurry to grow old

Lucille Ball

Mame (1974)

"The Anti-Mame"

I t's not worth expending too much time worrying about, but it is a puzzlement why once *I Love Lucy* left the air much of Lucille Ball's impeccable timing and exuberance seemed to have abandoned her. *The Lucy Show* got under way in 1962, just a few years after the Ricardos and the Mertzes had called it a day, but, with her voice deepening, her physical movements becoming strained, and her line readings turning arch, reconciling the Lucy of the new program with the comedy genius on the old was already a difficult proposition. Things only worsened as *The Lucy Show* (and, subsequently, *Here's Lucy*) ran season after season, and her antics became more and more ossified. If she hadn't remained fabulously rich and immensely popular with people who watched television, Ball's transformation as she got older would have been tragic. Instead, it was merely unfortunate.

Unfortunate, too, was what the actress did to Mame Dennis. In 1958's *Auntie Mame*, Rosalind Russell re-created her stage role as the warmhearted, sophisticated, and sometimes farcically hapless free-thinker who instills in her young nephew Patrick an open mind, inquisitiveness, and a sense of adventure. Hers was one of the screen's most irresistible and stylish comic performances. The vehicle became a Jerry Herman Broadway musical in 1966, providing a triumph for Angela Lansbury and reinventing her persona from harridanesque character-actress to chic leading lady. Despite her nearly three-decade screen career—and three Oscar nominations—when it came time for a film version of *Mame*, Lansbury became a

Looking like she's hepped up on Vitameatavegamin, Lucille Ball tries to shave off thirty years by having a go at a Charleston.

victim of the Hollywood rubric that, Roz Russell and a few others notwithstanding, the Broadway originator shall not recreate the role in the movie.

Doing publicity for *Mame*, Lucille Ball insisted that when she was approached for the movie, she "tried to talk them into signing Angela Lansbury for the title role. But Angela would have nothing to do with it. I guess she had her fill of the part." When Lansbury got wind of this, she responded, "I honestly don't know where Lucy ever got such an idea. I wanted to make the film of *Mame* in the worst way. But I was, quite simply, never asked." (But then again, Lucy was saying lots of odd things while tubthumping for *Mame*. She was pleased that her movie was rated G, "not X, like the kids are going to today." What did she have against those films that the young people enjoyed? "I think it's terrible that so many kids can see that explicit stuff. Even at age eighteen, youngsters see too much too soon in motion pictures. And I'm talking about boys as well as girls. It gives males a sense of inadequacy. They look at the herculean exploits and say: 'Oh, my God, there must be something wrong with me!'")

Lucille Ball was so wrong for *Mame* in so many ways. If her speaking voice had become husky, her singing was downright guttural, as though she had been dubbed by Tom Waits. Plus she couldn't carry a tune. Her dubious rebuttal to all those who panned her vocalizing was, "Mame drank and stayed up all night. Was she supposed to sound like Julie Andrews? *Come on!*" In any of its incarnations, the story of Auntie Mame is obviously a showcase for its female lead, but with Rosalind Russell the movie became the most egalitarian of star vehicles. Because Mame *just adores* and encourages creative, interesting people, Russell—emulating her character's sensibility—would generously step back and let members of her wonderful supporting cast to take center stage, allowing the film to become an ensemble piece. In *Mame*, Lucy is the whole show, riding roughshod over everyone else, as though she were filming an extended episode of *Here's Lucy*. The difference between the two approaches is that while Russell's Mame loves the world, Ball's is determined to *be loved* by it. Ironically, Ball comes across as harsh and unappealing, whereas Russell is warm and, well, lovable. Mugging mercilessly, Lucy's acting is much too broad, her timing way off, and *Mame*, like her concurrent television series, is painful for anyone who reveres *I Love Lucy*.

The title character is supposedly at the cusp of middle age when *Mame*—which covers about a dozen years—begins. Ball was sixty-one during filming, but she looked much older and seemed almost frail. Anytime she engages in slapstick hijinks (furiously clinging to a wild horse during a fox hunt, roller-skating through a department store), you feel anxious about her safety; hell, even while she's dancing you worry. Director Gene Saks—and likely the star herself—was aware of the age discrepancy between actress and character because, in a desperate ploy to hide her wrinkles, Ball was photographed with so many filters it seemed as though cinematographer Philip Lathrop had slathered Vaseline all over his camera lens. And not just in her close-ups but every time she's on-screen. As a result, you only become all the more aware of the actress's inapposite age. Moreover, any actor sharing a scene with her gets enveloped by this distracting soft focus miasma as well. Whenever he steps into the blurry aura surrounding Ball, Kirby Furlong—the mechanical ten-year-old playing young Patrick—resembles a fetus.

It's not simply the participation of Lucille Ball—*Mame* is awful in almost every particular. In the original versions of *Auntie Mame*, Mame faces antagonism from reactionary stuffed-shirts for trying to instill her nephew with progressive attitudes and exposing him to le dernier cri in intellectual and artistic thought; her outlandishness went only so far as schooling Patrick in the art of making a martini. Here, she takes Patrick sky diving, brings him to speakeasies and burlesque houses, and makes him perch with her atop the Statue of Liberty. Ball's Mame was clearly endangering the welfare of a child and she should have been arrested without delay.

Leslie Howard and Norma Shearer

Romeo and Juliet (1936)

"Middle-Age Crazy"

In *The Merchant of Venice*, Shakespeare wrote, "But love is blind, and lovers cannot see/The pretty follies that themselves commit." Case in point, MGM production supervisor Irving G. Thalberg. Unable to perceive the limitations of his movie star wife, he went ahead and cast her as a teenager in love. A rose by any other name would smell as sweet, and Norma Shearer going by the moniker of Juliet Capulet was still a thirty-three-year-old woman who did not even remotely suggest a thirteen-year-old with raging hormones.

To doubters who suggested that he might want to rethink his casting decision, an indignant Thalberg insisted that "Juliet can be any age" and besides, "Norma can play anything and do it better than anyone else." For studio head Louis B. Mayer, it was not so much the casting of Shearer as the project itself that was bothersome; his gut instinct was that moviegoers would have scant interest in an old play in which the characters didn't even speak like modern Americans. Mayer had visions of $2 million going down the drain because of Thalberg's pipe dream, but he grudgingly went along when Nicholas Schenck, president of the studio's parent company, got Thalberg to swear that the production would be brought in for $900,000.

Leslie Howard, who played Romeo, was even older than Shearer: a laughable forty-two. Initially uninterested because he contended that Romeo was one of Shakespeare's more insipid creations, Howard felt that the playwright "had his heart and soul in Juliet," while her boyfriend "seems hardly to be a three-dimensional figure; his principal function is to be the object of Juliet's affection." When Jack Warner refused to loan

A couple of kids in love.

him to MGM for the role, however, Howard suddenly decided that he was incensed. How dare this man deprive him of performing in a classic just because it was being made by another studio. A deal was worked out.

Thalberg did all he could to ensure that *Romeo and Juliet* was a class act. The film was assigned to one of the more cultivated directors in town, George Cukor, and Agnes DeMille was shipped in from the world of New York modern dance to create some fifteenth-century two-steps. Norma Shearer had had no formal training as an actress, so several *tres distingués* diction coaches were corralled to clue her in on the way of talking like a proper tragedienne. (Shearer drove her costar crazy with endless run-throughs of different phrasings. "This can go on forever," groaned Howard in the middle of filming, complaining that Shearer was "too serious about this part. The public won't mind whether she says 'Wherefore *art* thou, Romeo,' or '*Wherefore* art thou, Romeo,' and who cares, anyway?")

Before Norma Shearer appears on-screen, crusty old C. Aubrey Smith as Lord Capulet avers, "My child is yet a stranger in the world." The sentiment proves ridiculous because a few minutes later she shows up looking positively middle-aged, hardly passing for her actual thirty-three, never mind thirteen. Cukor used a form of smoke and mirrors in an attempt to counter the physical effects of the years upon Shearer. In her first appearance in the film, he has her feeding a deer, gambling that if she behaves like a kid at a petting zoo, the audience might just be fooled into thinking that she actually was a young thing. Even if the age difference between actress and character were not problematic, there were still Shearer's limitations as an actress. To convey youthfulness, she plasters a wide grin on her face, making Juliet seem less like an innocent girl than the village half-wit. Her physical movements are studied and mannered, most annoyingly her habit of abruptly jerking her head as if suddenly startled by something—a gaffer dropping a lamp offstage?—though, in actuality, this was her chosen means of expressing Juliet's beguilement at her burgeoning romance.

Throughout it all, Shearer has an unappetizing self-satisfaction that is antithetical to the role, most notably in the ball scene: Making her way among the party-goers, she expresses no sense of wonderment or enchantment at attending her first grown-up function. Rather, she marches with the haughty bearing of a Grande Dame, as if she were unable to shake the knowledge that she was *Norma Shearer, Queen of the MGM Lot*, and these people around her mere supporting players and extras. In the balcony scene, she's all breathiness and smirks, and for her big dramatic moments, such as when she hears that her lover has killed Tybalt, she really gets out of control, like a child on a sugar high. And although the studio sent out publicity releases about how accurate the film was to its period ("A Botticelli painting inspired the dress worn by Norma Shearer in her first scene with Leslie Howard"), Norma's hair is permed.

Then there's Leslie Howard. He's introduced to us in a sheep field, dewy-eyed and languid as he pines over his lost love, Rosalind. Such carryings-on are unseemly for a middle-aged man with a receding hairline. Howard's greatest deficiency is his lack of ardor, although, admittedly, making heartfelt such lines as, "Oh, she doth teach the torches to burn bright . . . I ne'er saw true beauty 'til this night" was an Augean task, considering that the object of his affection was Norma Shearer, she with the turned eye. So dispassionate is Howard's Romeo that one gets the feeling that if he couldn't have Juliet, he'd simply go out and woo another bachelorette.

Much of the supporting cast is as bad as the leads. Playing the impetuous Mercutio, fifty-four-year-old John Barrymore was frequently blotto on the set, which led him to give a performance that was all eye-popping and exaggerated elocution. His characterization is not that of an effervescent youth but of a crazed old man. Also on hand was the gravel-voiced, hayseed comic actor Andy Devine. Twenty years later Devine would become a cherished cultural icon for a whole generation of children when he would tell Froggy the Gremlin, "Twang your magic twanger!" on the *Andy's Gang* TV show. But no matter how much affection one may have for good old Andy, to hear him braying Shakespeare, even in the small comic relief role of the Capulet servant Peter, is unnerving.

Cukor had the actors recite the dialogue almost entirely as prose, not verse, so that the film scarcely feels like Shakespeare. Playing Tybalt, Basil Rathbone was the same age as John Barrymore but because he was the sole cast member who conveyed any sense of poetry, one overlooks his generational inappropriateness.

This movie fairly well defines high-minded kitsch. When the Montague gang breaks into song on their way to a party, you half expect Nelson Eddy to pop up with a chorus of "Stout-Hearted Men." The balcony scene is punctuated by strains of—what else?—Tchaikovsky's "Romeo and Juliet," and when the pair later consummate their marriage, another refrain of the ballet rises in crescendo as Cukor's camera pans away from the lovers to dreamy images of the stars, a frog pond, a flower garden, and finally the sun rising the next morning. Then we see that the duo is still fully clothed with Romeo lying against Juliet's bed, both feet firmly planted on the floor, the better to please the Hays Office.

MGM's publicity chief, Howard Dietz, had argued against the project from the beginning since it was *his* department that had to shoulder the responsibility of devising an ad campaign for *Romeo and Juliet* and convince the public that the movie was indeed entertainment and not the cinematic equivalent of castor oil. Don't worry, assured Thalberg. "With Norma it'll be a cinch." Advertisements for the film promised such attractions as "1,000 Things to See!" "Thrill After Thrill," and a "Love Story Supreme," the poster art emphasizing a duel between Howard and Rathbone so that filmgoers might be duped into believing that this was a swashbuckler among the lines of *Captain Blood*. Dietz also went for broke and in some advertisements lied that Shearer is "acclaimed the greatest Juliet of all times."

Romeo and Juliet opened in special high-priced engagements (with a $2.00 top) in large cities where it was intended to draw members of, in *Variety*'s parlance, "a new crop of cinema patrons from the arty, cultural, literate and dramatic bunch." The film did only moderately well in these venues, and when it was time for its second run at regular prices around the country—where it played on double bills with movies having titles like *Mama Steps Out*—the advertising department tried different ways of selling the film to the masses. These new ads ranged from the prurient ("One Night of Bliss. Wrestling happiness from jealous Fate under cover of darkness these two secretly wed lovers dared the wrath and dangers of a hostile world for one ecstatic night!") to soap opera ("To every woman who has ever known the triumphs and sorrows of love—she brings her heart-stabbing story") to the socially relevant ("A Boy and a Girl In Love . . . Separated by the Hatred of Their Parents . . . A Story As Modern As Today!"). There was even an attempt to sell the motion picture as an aphrodisiac: In a cartoon drawing, a taxi is listing precariously to its side. A word-balloon from inside the cab says, "This is *so* sudden." To which the frisky response from the other side of the taxi is, "You can't blame me after seeing *Romeo and Juliet*!"

It was all for naught: the movie never came close to recouping its cost. And poor Louis B. Mayer never got much of a chance to gloat in front of MGM's Boy Wonder. Two-and-a-half weeks after *Romeo and Juliet* premiered, Thalberg bit the dust at age thirty-seven. It would be another sixteen years before MGM again touched Shakespeare—and then *Julius Caesar* came about only after Louis B. Mayer had been given the boot from the studio.

Bernadette Peters

Slaves of New York (1989)

"Arrested Development"

The heroine of Tama Janowitz's only-in-the-eighties-could-it-have-been-a-success collection of stories, *Slaves of New York*, is a sweet young jewelry designer caught up in the downtown art scene and saddled with a creep of a boyfriend. In the Merchant-Ivory adaptation (talk about the unexpected), Eleanor has become a hat designer (oh, well—poetic license and no big deal) played by Bernadette Peters (oh, no!—producer's prerogative and a big mistake).

The crises that befall Eleanor—which center on launching a career and finding that most elusive of objects, a permanent relationship—are quintessential for people in their late twenties and early thirties. When she played Eleanor in *Slaves of New York*, Bernadette Peters was pushing forty-five. Although the actress's basic schitck continued to be her pouty little girl act, Peters was beginning to look a bit long in the tooth to bring it off. For her to be impersonating a wide-eyed innocent discovering the wherefore and whys of adulthood is a mite indecorous: someone her age should know better by now.

Exacerbating matters is the fact that her churlish boyfriend, Stash, as played by Adam Coleman Howard, looks like a kid. The obvious difference in their ages—she could be his mother—may give you a queasy feeling. Why is this mature—in years, anyway—woman in an emotionally abusive relationship with a whiny, narcissistic boy? (A typical Stash comment to Eleanor: "What is it that I hate about you most?") There are all sorts of dark ramifications hovering under the surface that the film simply ignores, as it blithely pretends that Peters is a kid herself. She does her utmost to keep up that impression, with her tremulous, kewpie doll posturing, and

Slaves of New York would have you believe that these two women represented the cutting edge of downtown New York in the eighties. No way. Bernadette Peters and Mercedes Ruehl were just a couple of stage actresses slumming.

twittery acting style. (Peters talks such a blue streak that she seems like a flesh-and-blood run-on sentence.) But to little avail. When Eleanor finally breaks away from Stash, bitterly telling him, "You don't have any feelings. You don't care about anybody," it's not the triumphant coming-of-age moment it's meant to be. Her emancipation is too long overdo.

Age isn't the only problem with Peters's casting. *Slaves of New York* takes place in the SoHo-TriBeCa–Lower East Side axis during the mid-1980s, when the "downtown scene" was at its peak. This was a world populated largely by artists (and would-be artists), performers, and hangers-on who created an insular society with its own codes of behavior and its own celebrities—and which Janowitz mocked even though she was in the thick of it. (It's been posited that this universe below 14th Street was made up of people who were decidedly not part of the In Group while growing up and were now attempting to thrive in an environment in which *they* were the arbiters of cool. Out of which was born the phrase, "tragically hip.")

Having been on the stage since she was a kid and a star since the late sixties, Bernadette Peters is, above all, a Broadway Baby. A musical-comedy performer of the old school, Peters exudes show-biz glitz, and while the downtown art world certainly had its theatrical aspects, they were of a different sort from the theatre's: stylized angst as opposed to smile-through-your-tears cockeyed optimism. You could perhaps picture Peters going below Canal Street out of anthropological curiosity or to have dinner at whichever restaurant was the hot eating spot *that* week. But the vulnerability that constitutes the essence of her waiflike persona is at odds with the posturing and self-consciously jaded attitude that were as de rigueur in Lower Manhattan as all-black outfits. Although the movie makes clear that Eleanor has not found fulfillment in this atmosphere, you wonder what she's doing there in the first place. (Bernadette Peters is Joe Allen's, not Odeon.) An inherent problem with *Slaves of New York* is that Janowitz wanted it both ways. She exploited the atmosphere of "downtown" by giving her readership a peek at an "exotic" locale, but did so through the eyes of an old-fashioned heroine with middle-class values and with whom the general public might identify. The mix didn't work in the book and it doesn't work in the movie.

Director James Ivory—renowned for his tasteful adaptations of period British novels—is as out of place downtown as Bernadette Peters is. Other movies from the period set in this milieu (Susan Seidelman's *Desperately Seeking Susan*, Martin Scorsese's *After Hours*, and Jonathan Demme's *Something Wild*) were atmospheric works made by directors who knew the terrain. *Slaves of New York* has the feel of TriBeCa as seen from a tour bus, overflowing as it is with determinedly "outrageous" characters whom you don't believe for a second. With Tama Janowitz's help, Ivory came up with the cinematic equivalent of a party with the guest list from hell. You can't wait to get out.

Barbra Streisand

Hello, Dolly! (1969)

"Misspent Youth"

When *Hello, Dolly!* opened on Broadway in January 1964, New York had its biggest hit since *My Fair Lady* eight years earlier. At the center of Jerry Herman's high-spirited musical adaptation of Thornton Wilder's comedy *The Matchmaker* was Carol Channing. As Dolly Levi, the exuberant marriage-broker and professional meddler, Channing received praise that bordered on the idolatrous. Soon after, the show's producer, David Merrick, announced that he would be producing the movie version of *Hello, Dolly!*, with his star reprising her celebrated performance.

The next year, Merrick sold the film rights to 20th Century–Fox, and Carol Channing had cause for worry. Although she was still under consideration, Fox's production chief Richard Zanuck acknowledged that Doris Day, Shirley MacLaine, and Julie Andrews were all being given the once-over. Later the buzz was that Elizabeth Taylor had the inside track. No one could make the argument that Channing had an impressive list of films on her resumé: there were only two and they weren't exactly classics. She had had a tiny part in a 1950 soap opera, *Paid in Full*, and in *The First Traveling Saleslady*, a 1956 flop comedy Western, Channing had played second banana to Ginger Rogers and her love interest was pre-*Rawhide* Clint Eastwood.

With plans for the *Hello, Dolly!* movie still up in the air, Channing had a costarring role with Julie Andrews in *Thoroughly Modern Millie*, a Roaring Twenties musical that provided a showcase for her particular brand of brassiness. The movie was very popular, and Channing received good reviews, but in terms of serving as a *Hello, Dolly!* screen test, *Thoroughly Modern Millie* backfired. The one person most crucial to her

Why are these people laughing?

immediate future was underwhelmed. "I thought Carol Channing was a little grotesque, cartoonish," said Ernest Lehman, writer-producer of the film version of *Hello, Dolly!*

Granted, Carol Channing was no movie star. But then, in May of 1967, the studio announced that the part of Dolly Levi would be played by a woman who had made even fewer films than Channing, in fact, none. Despite a lack of cinematic credits, however, Barbra Streisand, with her mannered histrionics, commanded an obsessive, almost cultlike following. Streisand's celebrity arose from records, nightclub and television appearances, and two Broadway shows, most notably *Funny Girl*, in which she played comedienne Fannie Brice. (Ironically, *Funny Girl* opened during the 1963–64 season and was mowed down at the Tonys by *Hello, Dolly!*; the Best Actress—Musical star winner was not Streisand but Carol Channing.)

Criticism of Streisand's casting was immediate and intense; Richard L. Coe, drama critic of the *Washington Post*, called the decision "knuckleheaded." Channing's advocates protested that simple logic and fair play mandated that just as Streisand had been signed to do the film version of *Funny Girl*, so should the *Hello, Dolly!* star be given the opportunity to recreate her stage success. On top of it all, this shoddy treatment of Channing by Fox was nothing new. Back in 1953, the studio had deprived her of a shot at screen stardom by handing over her signature role as the diamond-loving golddigger Lorelei Lee in *Gentlemen Prefer Blondes* to Marilyn Monroe.

With *Hello, Dolly!* there was not only the issue of Streisand's own lack of experience, but, more important, her complete and utter unsuitability for the role, by any reasonable, objective standard. The character of Dolly Levi is a middle-aged widow, a seasoned, worldy-wise woman who has spent years grieving for her husband and is just now reemerging into society, ready to land a new beau. Channing was forty-three when she opened in *Hello, Dolly!*, and even she was considered on the youngish side for the part. (Ruth Gordon was fifty-nine when she appeared in *The Matchmaker*, and Shirley Booth starred in the film version at fifty-one). When filming started, Streisand was twenty-five. In the stage musical, it is spelled out that Dolly has been out of commission for ten years, which, in Streisand's case would have meant she was widowed at age fifteen—a child bride.

It didn't add any years to Streisand's Dolly by having other characters refer to her as "the old girl"—it only made them seem like idiots. In the original play, Dolly is often referred to by her maiden name, Gallagher. Ernest Lehman and director Gene Kelly may have tried to fudge the age issue, but even they realized that playing Irish would be too great an acting stretch, so Streisand is plain and simply Levi.

Ernest Lehman would have benefited from listening to the protestors. On-screen, Dolly Levi became equal parts Mae West and Barbra Streisand, with traces of a southern accent also thrown in from time to time (pretty weird for a character who is a native New Yorker). The star was roundly panned. *Time* felt that "her mannerisms are so arch and calculated that one half-expects to find a key implanted in her back," and the *Hollywood Citizen News* complained that "Miss Streisand's Dolly is overshadowed by a 'Yiddish Mama' characterization that subdues and stifles the vivacious loquacity that was the particular charm of the stage Dolly."

Indeed, her matchmaker seems less Dolly Levi than Yente, the marriage fixer of *Fiddler on the Roof*. There is no longer anything affecting about this character, whose joie de vivre and puckish humor have been replaced by steely determination.

The lack of rapport between Streisand and Walter Matthau, who played the wealthy merchant the Widow Levi hopes to hook, came as no surprise, given all the gossip about the tension between the two of them on the set. Appalled by what he deemed her "megalomania," Matthau at one point told Streisand, "Nobody in this company likes you." When she stormed off the set, he hollered after her, "Go ahead. But remember Betty Hutton thought she was indispensable, too."

The most expensive musical up to that time, *Hello, Dolly!* is also one of the worst. It is gargantuan, but it remains an empty vessel in which the overblown sets and production numbers have drained all signs of life: commotion and hubbub seem to be its raison d'être, with actors bellowing to compete with the prodigiousness surrounding them. One's tolerance for *Hello, Dolly!* will be in direct ratio to one's tolerance for Streisand in her brash, unmodulated youthful period—or as a nonfan might put it, when her act was not so much singing as it was haranguing with music.

Hello, Dolly! did attract crowds of patrons, but not nearly enough for 20th Century–Fox to recoup its investment. Carol Channing saw the film and said of Streisand, "I thought she did the best job she could do." Channing had been touring with the show in Montreal back in 1967 when she learned that the screen version of *Hello, Dolly!* would not be hers. She waxed philosophic that "four years is probably long enough to stay with one part" and "so we'll close the book on *Dolly*." As it turned out, thirty-one years after first appearing in the musical, Channing took *Hello, Dolly!* to Broadway for the third time, having toured with various productions of the show for ages. On opening night 1995 she was playing the role of Dolly Gallagher Levi for close to the 4,500th time.

AN ERROR IN ERAS

*Performers whose personas and modern sensibilities were
completely out of place when they traveled to the past*

Pat Boone and John Wayne

The Greatest Story Ever Told (1965)

"Good Book Goes Bad"

Coming three and a half years after *King of Kings*, George Stevens's *The Greatest Story Ever Told* was another cinematic retelling of the life of Jesus. A reporter for the *New York Times* mused that "it is perhaps ironic that Stevens had chosen to produce a morality play at a time when many Americans movies seem preoccupied with smut." Making sure everyone knew that his film was taking the high road, the producer-director made pronouncements unto the press, such as, "If we take the story from the Bible we find no swordplay and very little other film excitements such as bacchanals. The story of Jesus is strong stuff without that." Stevens even roped in poet Carl Sandburg for the project (as "creative consultant"). At the time you couldn't get any more distinguished than that.

The producer-director said that he had "seen something of Jesus suggested in certain of Marlon Brando's scenes in *On the Waterfront*," but ultimately Max von Sydow, from the Ingmar Bergman stock company, was cast as Christ. (Originally von Sydow had no interest in playing the role because "I thought with horror of Cecil B. DeMille and such things as *Samson and Delilah* and *The Ten Commandments*. But when I saw the script, I decided that the role of Jesus is absolutely not a religious cliché.") After Stevens suggested to *Variety* that Audrey Hepburn would make a great Virgin Mary, the newspaper wondered if putting big-name actors into small roles might not prove a distraction. The "best actors are

Roman finery does not suit John Wayne nearly as well as do his traditional dungarees, chaps, gun belt, and kerchief. And that helmet is no substitute for a ten-gallon hat.

needed," responded the director. As it turned out, Hepburn was nowhere to be seen, but plenty of other A-list actors were on hand. For those of us who were kids at the time, the most exciting news was that Illya Kuryakin (David McCallum) was in the film, even if he was playing that rotten Judas Iscariot.

Most reviewers were well disposed toward *The Greatest Story Ever Told*, praising it for the sobersided qualities George Stevens had been touting, even if they found the film a little ponderous. Admirers approved of the film more for what it had avoided than for anything in particular within it. *Variety* commented that Stevens "has scorned plot gimmicks and scanted on characterization quirks. There are no neurotic kings, no chariot races, no tortures, no necrophilic foamings over a man's head served on a platter to a crazy, mixed up, hot country girl. There is a veil dance but it could be presented at a parish tea."

But even its most ardent fans castigated Stevens for his all-star casting. *Los Angeles* magazine scoffed that "it seemed outrageous to see a Charlton Heston, José Ferrer, or Sal Mineo behind every olive tree. . . . One wastes an inordinate amount of time consciously and unconsciously trying to spot or recognize stars one knows to be in the film." Among others making appearances are Dorothy McGuire, who replaced Audrey Hepburn as Mary (and doesn't say a single word during the entire four-hour running time); Claude Rains as Herod the Great; Angela Lansbury as Mrs. Pontius Pilate; and Carroll Baker as Veronica, who wipes Jesus's face while He is carrying the cross (at the same time Baker was titillating audiences in movies like *The Carpetbaggers* and *Harlow*, thus mixing the sacred and the profane). Sidney Poitier, tall and dignified as he voluntarily helps the white Jesus carry the cross, is a perfect Simon of Cyrene for the Civil Rights era.

The Greatest Story Ever Told seems all the more "all-star" today because it features several actors who were not readily identifiable to the average moviegoer in 1965 but later became television stars: *Baretta*'s Robert Blake; *Mission: Impossible*'s Martin Landau; Russell Johnson, the Professor in *Gilligan's Island*; and, most amusingly of all, Jamie Farr, the dress-wearing Corporal Klinger from *M*A*S*H*, as one of the apostles.

The cameos in *The Greatest Story Ever Told* are nutty, but they're also the most enjoyable thing about the film (although von Sydow is probably about as good as any actor playing Jesus could be). This pharaonic

Pat Boone brings his all-American wholesomeness to the Middle East when he breaks the news to Mary Magdalene (Joanna Dunham) that Jesus has left His tomb on Easter morning. (Photofest)

movie is slow, stately, and solemn. Seeing familiar faces—a precursor to *Where's Waldo*—livens things up considerably. Waiting in anticipation for an Ed Wynn to show up is like being a kid sitting in Sunday school or catechism class, inordinately bored, and hoping that two girls will get caught passing notes and the teacher will make them read them out loud, or else some other kid will get sick and throw up before being able to rush out of the classroom—little moments that add spice to an otherwise deadly morning.

No matter how amenable you may be to seeing some of your old favorites in *The Greatest Story Every Told*, there are two cameos that test the limits of one's tolerance. On Easter morning, when Mary Magdalene arrives at Christ's tomb, she sees, in accordance with the prophecies, not Jesus's body but Pat Boone. Boone has traded in his white bucks for sensible desert sandals, his cover versions of rhythm and blues records for the Scriptures, but he's still got that sickeningly wholesome, all-American boyish charm. Pat has a mere three lines. "He is gone," he tells Mary Magdalene. "Why seek ye the living among the dead? He is risen." A devout Christian, Boone must have busted his britches at being the one who gets to announce that Jesus's resurrection is a reality—although, with Handel's "Hallelujah Chorus" booming on the soundtrack, Boone's soft-spoken line readings make it a little difficult to hear all fourteen of his words clearly.

In a performance second only to his Genghis Khan as a career low point, John Wayne is on hand as the Roman Centurion. During the Carrying of the Cross, Wayne walks disinterestedly behind Jesus, not mocking, striking, or scourging Him. (John Wayne assault the Lord? No way.) And when Christ gets to Calvary, Duke doesn't join in the hammering of the nails into His hands and feet or setting up the Cross. He stands stage right during the Crucifixion, merely an observer, his cape billowing in the wind. Stevens photographs him in medium shots, with the camera pointing up toward him, making him look majestic and imbuing the Centurion with that old John Wayne heroic stance.

When Jesus dies and a thunderstorm kicks up, Wayne has his one line: "Truly, this man was the Son of God." The actor mutters the sentiment, not sounding entirely convinced, although his unmistakable cadence comes through. A story has passed down from the set of *The Greatest Story Ever Told* and, although it may well be apocryphal, you want to believe it. Not completely satisfied after hearing several takes, Stevens told Wayne, "We need something more in the scene. Look at the man on the Cross and give us some . . . some awe." Wayne indicated that he understood. On the next take he said, "Awww, truly this was the Son of God."

Robert De Niro

The Mission (1986)

"A Latin From Manhattan"

In Roland Joffe's *The Mission*, Robert De Niro is a Spaniard named Rodrigo Mendoza, whose home base is a rain forest in South America in the 1750s. The actor is equally inept at conveying a sense of time and a sense of place.

Rodrigo is a slaver whose fiancée has fallen for someone else. This state of affairs provides De Niro with the comic highlight of *The Mission*: he says to Carlotta, "So me you do not love?" Rodrigo adores his kid brother but kills him anyway, in a fit of jealousy, for it was him she did love. It's remorse time, and when the local Jesuit, Father Gabriel (Jeremy Irons), gets ahold of him, Rodrigo is feeling awfully bad, not just about his dead brother but about all the Indians he's killed and sold into slavery. His penance isn't a run-of-the-mill three Our Fathers and three Hail Mary's. Instead, Father Gabriel has him dragging a huge collection of heavy armor supplies up the side of a mountain to a remote Jesuit mission. Rodrigo apparently gets off on the pain and humiliation, for he decides to hang around the mission, and the next thing you know, he's a full-fledged priest.

The Rodrigo–Father Gabriel relationship is the intimate aspect of the movie. The significant-because-it-has-parallels-to-our-own-troubled-times aspect has to do with an arcane conflict involving the Spanish, the Portuguese, and the Church, and dealing with South American real estate. The end result is that the native Guarani Indians who had converted to Catholicism will again be enslaved by the Portuguese. Father Gabriel isn't particularly pleased about things, but he's of the "Thy will be done" school and offers no resistance. Rodrigo, however, reverts to his man-

Robert De Niro strikes a pose in an early version of voguing.

of-action posture and leads a revolt. The moral of *The Mission* is that it was bad of the imperialist Europeans to subjugate the Indians of South America and for the Catholic Church to have turned a blind eye. Well, duh.

Nearly every review of *The Mission* dwelled upon how out of place De Niro's New York–tinged maunderings were in this movie. Vincent Canby of the *New York Times* felt that he "is all right here until he opens his mouth." In addition to the previously mentioned inquiry of his affianced, he is particularly piquant with the line, "About women, I'm always right, you know that." (If this movie did nothing else, it announced to the world that Robert De Niro should never be handed dialogue in which the normal order of words has been given a poetic scramble.) And why didn't the actor or his direc-tor (or one of the best boys, for that matter) immediately realize that when, fretting that others know about his romantic travails, Rodrigo approaches people with an accusatory "You laughing at me?" it could only be taken as a parody of *Taxi Driver*'s "You talkin to me?" (Jeremy Irons has an easier time of it than De Niro, partially because his aesthete qualities are well suited to the beatific Father Gabriel, and also be-cause over the years the movies have accustomed us to accepting British accents in practically any setting, even the jungles of South America. Irons does make an ass of himself though when he's saddled with an anguished, "If might is right, then love has no place in the world. It may be so, it may be so."

In the second part of the film, when Rodrigo marshals the Indians into armed resistance, De Niro is still all wrong, but for different reasons. Guerrilla warfare calls for an action hero, someone who moves with physical aplomb. (This is very likely the only thing in the world Sylvester Stallone can do better than De Niro.) De Niro may be menacing as a New York hood or a psycho roaming the mean streets, but when he's charging through the jungle and shooting a musket he's in the wrong arena. Plus, he's doing his back-to-nature macho bit while wearing a monk's robe. Running around in a long garment like that could really trip you up.

Demi Moore

The Scarlet Letter (1995)

"Naked in New England"

Why do people set themselves up for such an obvious and easy fall? Coming off a couple of self-important bombs—*Fat Man and Little Boy* and *City of Joy*—director Roland Joffe should have been more circumspect. But no, he had to open his trap and say that Nathaniel Hawthorne's *The Scarlett Letter*—which would likely be cited as the Great American Novel by literary critics as frequently as any other book—was a "badly thought-out polemic against adultery" which had been "gathering dust on the shelves." Other times, Joffe's choice of words was more prudent, but in his new role as literature professor/psychoanalyst he always came to the same conclusion: It was time for a rewrite of the 1850 novel.

Discussing literature's most famous adulteress and her creator, Joffe said, "Hawthorne is clearly so in love with Hester Prynne but he is also terrified by her. The whole book seems to yearn to set her free, but ultimately, Hawthorne can't. He has pinned Hester like a butterfly and I thought it would be wonderful to pull the pin out of her and let her fly." In other words, Joffe wanted a woman of the nineties. Demi Moore may not have been conceivable to Nathaniel Hawthorne, but she certainly fit the bill for Roland Joffe's "improvements."

Discussing the star of *Ghost* and *Indecent Proposal*, Joffe said, "Here is a woman who has taken charge of her own life. She has all the spirit of Hester, consistent with an earthiness, a mixture of intelligence, modesty, and sensuality that I felt was close to the character." And as though that all wasn't enough, "There is that spark of mischief and sense of humor which I felt would allow Demi to connect with Hester on a visceral level," although levity is not one of the traits that immediately

Shame, shame, everybody knows your name. The scorn endured by Hester Prynne was nothing compared to the ridicule heaped upon Demi Moore and everyone else involved with *The Scarlet Letter.*

springs to mind when one thinks of Hawthorne's Hester Prynne.

Demi was right in sync with her director and his screenwriter. When word got out that Joffe and scripter Douglas Day Stewart—best known for *An Officer and a Gentleman,* but also the writer of the 1980 version of *The Blue Lagoon,* in which a nice Victorian novel was tarted up as a Brooke Shields sex show—had revamped the novel to give it a happy ending, the response was incredulous laughter. The leading lady didn't see what all the fuss was about: "Not many people have read the book," said Demi Moore.

Joffe and Stewart seemed to feel that Hawthorne's novel was a gyp: opening with Hester receiving her scarlet *A,* it gives you the punishment but not the sin. So for an hour, the movie details their version of what went on a priori, i.e., all the good stuff. We see Demi (we'll call her Demi, because despite her name, this character certainly isn't Hester Prynne) getting her mojo working while she watches local minister Arthur Dimmesdale (Gary Oldman, sporting a Generation X goatee) happily skinny-dipping. In their next encounter the two of them are riding horses. The steady, rhythmic movements of a hot-blooded animal underneath her while she simultaneously has Arthur in her sights gets Demi hot and bothered pretty good. More foreplay for the audience: we see flashes of skin when Demi takes a bath and preens away, as water languidly flows over her breasts and her fingers go where a good Puritan damsel's fingers shouldn't.

Demi may be one libidinous babe, but she's also a true and faithful wife, even if her husband, Roger Chillingworth (Robert Duvall), is mean, old, and still back in England. When Demi gets word that she's now a widow, the Reverend Dimmesdale is soon seeing more than flashes of skin, and their Puritan bodies become as one on a highly romantic pile of feed grain. Their lovemaking not only liberates them from the shackles of seventeenth-century colonial society, it also has an intoxicating effect on the mute black servant girl who's been sneaking a peek at them. Also hovering around the scene is a symbolic red canary that makes guest appearances throughout the movie. Joffe and Stewart remain faithful to Hawthorne in one aspect: their Roger Chillingworth, like Hawthorne's, shows up alive, although in the novel he didn't dance around in the woods while wearing a dead animal on his head as if he had just read *Iron John* and was getting in touch with his maleness.

Even when the movie catches up to page one of the novel, it continues to be filled with flights of fancy. The Reverend Dimmesdale, a milksop in his original incarnation, is now a paragon for the 1990s—sensitive yes, but manly and decisive and strong; he's the kind of hale and hearty fellow who in his spare time tries to bring about peace and brotherhood between the local Indians and the settlers. Chillingworth is no longer a dull old sourpuss; now he's a man of action who goes out to scalp Dimmesdale, and if he got the wrong man, well these things happen. Demi fends off a rapist with a gun and an epithet: "You bastard!" which really shouldn't come tripping so readily off the tongue of a Puritan woman.

But who was kidding whom? You don't put Demi Moore into a period piece with the idea that an audience is going to be expecting verisimilitude. And it's impossible to build a believable movie around the idea of a woman's burgeoning sexuality, when that woman is played by an actress whose most noteworthy achievement was twice posing nude for the cover of *Vanity Fair*—once while eight months pregnant. A woman of modest talents, Moore has been portraying impassioned women on screen for so long now that she would probably be incapable of conveying a sexually repressed character even if she were fitted with a chastity belt.

Joffe and Stewart, however, did not call for a doubt-ridden Hester Prynne. Their leading character is a woman whose sensibility is from three hundred years in the future, a free-thinking feminist who has none of the shame and remorse of Hawthorne's Hester. As usual, the smirking Moore conveys a cocksure haughtiness and smug self-reverence, traits that mark her as a completely contemporary actress. Far from being a woman affected by the powerful societal influences of her particular environment,

Moore's Hester is a "Go for it!" type of gal from the outset, a characterization that makes no sense at all in seventeenth-century Massachusetts.

The infamous self-designed bicycle pants outfit she wore at the 1988 Oscars attests to Moore's sartorial taste: she's not going to be content wearing simple Puritan garb. When Demi is viewing Dimmesdale's nude bathing frolic, her hair is accessorized with an Earth Mother festoon of assorted fresh flowers. Her *A* is attached to a lace chemise smock that covers, and adds a chic quality to, her traditional pilgrim dress. Critic Dave Kehr referred to another, fancier, outfit as "a wasp-waisted ball gown that looks as if it had been designed by the Puritan Bob Mackie."

Come to think of it, those sweepingly asinine statements that Roland Joffe had made probably didn't matter. What he did to *The Scarlet Letter* would have made him a laughingstock even if he had sounded like Mark Van Doren in his publicity pronouncements. Everyone had his own favorite among the movie's many awful moments, but all were in agreement that the happy ending was particularly dumbfounding. It wasn't simply an upbeat denouement, but one brought about by an Indian attack that inadvertently frees Dimmesdale as he's facing the gallows. In Hawthorne's novel, the minister succumbs to his grief and guilt and dies, leaving Hester to spend the rest of her life in sorrowful solitude in Salem. It is only in death that Hester and Dimmesdale will be together. When the film closes, the two of them are driving off together to the Carolinas.

Soon after the movie opened, a cartoon in the *New Yorker* was captioned "Moby Dick: The Demi Moore Version." It showed a beaming Captain Ahab, the captured white whale hanging from a hook on one side, Demi clinging to him on the other. On *Leave It to Beaver*, the Beav once got himself into hot water because he based his book report about *The Three Musketeers* on the old movie version starring Don Ameche and the Ritz Brothers. Woe to the lazy student who writes a paper on *The Scarlet Letter* after seeing only what Roland Joffe and Demi Moore have done to it.

Al Pacino

Revolution (1985)

"Da Redcoats Are Comin'!"

It's doubtful that there was such a thing as a Bronx accent in 1776. This raises the question of why producer Irwin Winkler and director Hugh Hudson decided to engage Al Pacino, the foremost practitioner of New York speech patterns since Leo Gorcey, to play a Revolutionary War soldier. But once Pacino signed on for the project, it might have been a good idea for his director to insist that he—an actor of some talent—do something with his voice. And if Pacino wasn't going to try for authenticity in his speech, then writer Robert Dillon probably shouldn't have compounded the problem by giving his character dialogue containing the sort of double negatives (e.g., "You ain't blowing up no grenade, you hear? . . . You ain't going nowhere") that bring to mind juvenile delinquents from fifties social dramas and the goombahs who populate Martin Scorsese's Little Italy.

It's not simply the actor's "dem-and-dose" vocal stylings that are so jarring in the middle of colonial America—it's the entire mien of this most joyless of movie stars. Pacino's Tom Dobb is a Scottish-born trapper and supposedly a simple man of the land, but because the actor's patented brooding is on automatic pilot, the character becomes a morose soul mate of such purveyors of late-twentieth-century urban angst as Frank Serpico and *Dog Day Afternoon*'s Sonny ("Attica!") Wortzik. And, let's face it, the Sicilian hangdog look was not exactly common in the thirteen colonies. You could scrutinize all the collected paintings of Gilbert Stuart and John Singleton Copley and not find a single face that even approximates Pacino's.

Yankee Doodle Dandy Al Pacino demonstrates his understated acting style.

Beyond the incongruity of featuring Al Pacino handling a musket and wearing buckskin, *Revolution* is still a fiasco because it's a movie about the American War for Independence that doesn't have a clue as to what all the fuss was about. Director Hudson and writer Dillon chose to tell the story of the American Revolution through the events in one Average Joe's life; the problem is that if you have a hero who is inarticulate, not much of importance is going to get said. The movie won't jar any grammar school memories because there's no mention of the Stamp Act, the Intolerable Acts, the Boston Massacre, or any of the other things we studied in fourth grade history. Although the film opens on July 4, 1776, we're shown not the ratification of the Declaration of Independence but, instead, an unruly citizenry, presumably consumed by revolutionary fever though acting more like teenagers jumping into a mosh pit.

The film's hero is also apathetic to the goals of the colonists. Dobb's mantra is "It ain't my fight," and he only signs up with the Continental

Army to keep an eye on his impetuous (i.e., stupid) adolescent son Ned, who had joined up before him—a budding Gene Krupa, Ned found the idea of being in the fife and drum corps irresistible. Years pass, and, having left the army, Tom becomes a backwoods scout, an eighteenth-century Rambo who hangs out with the Indians and shadows the Redcoats. He hasn't belatedly embraced the cause of liberty, but rather has again been thrust into the middle of things because of his son. The kid was tortured nearly to death after sassing off to a pederast British officer who had fancied him, and that made Tom *really* mad. (Good thing the Dobbs weren't around in ancient Greece.)

Pacino does all of the standard Pacino things in *Revolution*—the scowling, the moping, the glowering, the mumbling, and the wailing and gnashing of teeth. So much technique, and none of it appropriate for the character he's playing. At least Goldcrest Films, the British company that bankrolled the movie, got its money's worth: it shelled out for an actor and Pacino gave back a lot of *acting* for the bucks.

Al Pacino is not the only anachronism in *Revolution*. Bewildered characters can be heard to mutter "What the hell?" and there are several references to the "American dream" at a time long before anyone salivated over the thought of two cars in the garage and a diversified stock portfolio. (*Webster's* informs us that the phrase first entered the vernacular in 1931). The dialogue at least is good for a few laughs, such as when Tory Joan Plowright is surrounded in her carriage by a group of July Fourth revelers, one of whom hands her daughter—Nastassja Kinski(!)—a copy of the brand new Declaration of Independence. (Who knew the printing presses and mails were so efficient in those days?) Plowright pulls the paper out of Kinski's hand and says, "Daisy, now don't you go spoiling our lovely day," then sighs, "The last thing I need today is a headache." *Revolution* also contains an incomparable (and probably unintentional) double entendre: Kinski, seeing that Pacino's son is now a strapping young man played by an older actor, comments, "You've grown! You've got your own rifle!"

A very expensive movie that was splattered with derisive reviews and lost a bundle, *Revolution* is up there with *Heaven's Gate*, *Howard the Duck*, and *Ishtar* as one of the unmitigated disasters of the 1980s. As to the question of why Pacino was cast as Tom Dobb (Richard Gere and

Robert Duvall had also been in the running), Hugh Hudson explained: Pacino's "from the South Bronx, and I wanted someone from the back streets of Glasgow, a street guy, a street *rat*. Al's from a deprived background, ten years ago he hadn't two pennies to rub together, and that quality comes off him still. He's really been through it." That was highly fallacious reasoning.

OUT OF THEIR LEAGUE

*Movie stars whose attempts at roles different
than those they usually played were stymied by either
a too strongly established screen persona
or simply by limited acting skills*

The jig is up, and America's one-time "girl next door" doesn't end up getting away with murder. The sweatshirt was June Allyson's idea of lesbian chic circa 1972, and note the smudge of dirt director James Goldstone insisted on putting on her cheek for verisimilitude. (Museum of Modern Art/Film Stills Archives)

June Allyson

They Only Kill Their Masters (1972)

"Psycho Sappho"

What used to be called "gay liberation" was a relatively new political movement in 1972, but from the evidence of *The Only Kill Their Masters*, a screenwriter named Lane Slate seemed awfully unnerved by it. The movie, in which James Garner plays the police chief of a small northern California town, is supremely inconsequential—everything about this murder mystery has the feel of a television show. If you can come across it while flipping through the channels, it would be a while before you realized it wasn't an episode of *The Rockford Files*.

A pregnant woman is found dead on the beach. Because her Doberman is found nearby, and the corpse has teeth marks on it, the pooch becomes the prime suspect. But the dog is innocent—the wounds indicate it was trying to *save* its master. If man's best friend didn't bring cold-blooded murder into a sleepy community, who did? A killer lesbian, naturally.

In this movie, the deadly dyke is the personification of the homosexual threat. Fear permeates *The Only Kill Their Masters*, which warns that "these people" could be anywhere. A pleasant evening at the local tavern is ruined when two leather-and-denim boys—a couple of nonlocals—start busting up the joint. The dead mother-to-be is herself revealed to have been a lesbian. "A pregnant lesbian? Isn't that a contradiction in terms?" asks veterinarian assistant Katharine Ross. "Well, city people," responds Garner. "Who knows what they do? What they want?" Yes. The murdered woman is from "the city." *They Only Kill Their Masters* is not just homophobic, it's also filled with an old-fashioned loathing of urban areas. For writer Slate in 1972, the city was the environs for "free love"—*Vari-*

ety referred to the movie's murder victim as "a swinger"—and these city folk were bent on polluting morally upright communities everywhere with their lascivious ways.

But, says the film, beware of the enemy within, too. Even an old shoe like James Garner. When he and Katharine Ross are exchanging background information as they become acquainted, Garner's police chief declares, "I'm a faggot." Oh, he's just kidding. But, then again, he's *not* married and he doesn't have kids, though he does make a mean meat loaf. The Freudians undoubtedly would have something to say about his little josh.

The film contains something even more shocking than the possible proclivities of James Garner's character. The murderous Sapphite is revealed to be Mrs. Watkins, the veterinarian's wife, but we know her as America's favorite girl-next-door, June Allyson. The warm and wonderful little lady who used to romance Van Johnson and comfort James Stewart with her irresistibly husky voice, a lesbian? And look at how her lifestyle has turned her cute-as-a-button-face hard and bitter. See, says *They Only Kill Their Masters*, if a woman played by June Allyson is a deviant, anyone might be. Lock up your wives and your daughters, and your sons.

But not so fast! Mrs. Watkins isn't a character at all, she's a plot device. We catch a very brief glimpse of her early in the film and then not again until she's arrested for murder. Because June Allyson isn't given any opportunity to build a character, when we see her on screen she remains nothing but June Allyson doing a cameo appearance. And the associations Allyson brings with her are of devoted sweethearts and loving wives, not a married lesbian who killed out of jealousy. She bitterly refers to her ex-lover as a "bitch," and she rambles on incoherently, damning the dead woman for not being satisfied with being part of a couple but insisting on recruiting Allyson's husband, Hal Holbrook, for a ménage à trois and later another man for a ménage à quatre. But she's still just June Allyson reading some sleazy lines. And neither her football sweatshirt nor her butch haircut—not even the smudge of dirt on her cheek—convinces us that this woman would have an "alternative lifestyle."

Humphrey Bogart

The Return of Dr. X (1939)

"Bloodsucker"

J ust because an actor specializes in villains doesn't mean he'll be equally adept at every type of villain there is. Movie heavies run the gamut from distinguished captains of industry to lowlifes who have climbed out from under a rock. Humphrey Bogart is a case in point. (It's the bad boy Bogie of the thirties under discussion here, before he became the seminal cynicism-encrusted, romantic idealist in *Casablanca* and *To Have and Have Not*.) Bogart in a double-breasted suit with a pistol in his hand is scary. Bogart entering the realm of Boris Karloff and Bela Lugosi as a sort of hybrid vampire-zombie is hilarious.

For the Bette Davis vehicle *The Old Maid*, Bogart initially had been assigned the relatively small but pivotal role of a dashing young man who knocks up Davis and then goes off and gets killed in the Civil War. Studio head Jack Warner saw the rushes and decided that Bogart wasn't the type for whom a woman would throw her life away. He gave that part to Davis's boiler plate leading man, George Brent, and, needing to keep him busy, stuck Bogart with the title role in *The Return of Dr. X.*

Although Bogart's character's name is Marshall Quesne, you can tell he's really Dr. X the first time you see him. Who else would have such a gaunt face, pasty skin, and humorless disposition, though God only knows what the shock of white in his buzz-cut mane was supposed to signify. This Quesne chap works as a lab assistant to brilliant hematologist John Litel, but the top-billed Wayne Morris—a reporter investigating a series of gruesome murders in which all the victims were drained of their blood—discovers the strange and shocking truth about the two men.

Hard to believe that a couple of years later this man would create one of the most indelibly romantic figures in the movies. But that's how it was under the studio system. One day you're the title character in *The Return of Dr. X*, the next you're starring in *Casablanca*.

Here's the scoop: Quesne used to be a certain Dr. Xavier, who was in his lab one day conducting a little experiment to see how long kids can go without eating. He wasn't paying close enough attention, and a baby under his watch died of starvation, which at least offered the doctor an answer to his query. Xavier was then electrocuted as a murderer. As a fellow scientist also doing oddball medical research, Dr. Litel took pity on Bogart's dead body and infused it with a synthetic blood he developed. The transfusion is successful, but there's one drawback: once you get this blood, you have an uncontrollable urge to replenish it with the real stuff. Hence the murders. Bogart's mistake is going after nurse Rosemary Lane, for if there's one thing we have learned from movies over the years, it's that you don't mess with the leading lady. In his laboratory somewhere out in the New Jersey meadowlands, Bogart is killed for a second and final time.

Even if you're willing to suspend your disbelief—as you always must for this genre—*The Return of Dr. X* can't possibly be taken seriously: Humphrey Bogart looks too silly. His clammy complexion is so overdone that it seems as though he stuck his face into a vat of powder before each take (and, besides, if he's constantly restocking his blood, shouldn't he be rosy-cheeked?). You didn't blink twice when Boris Karloff played these parts—in fact, Bogart's makeup was very clearly modeled on Karloff's "look" in *The Walking Dead* three years earlier, which was also a Warner Bros. movie—but Humphrey Bogart should be shaking down nightclub owners and double-crossing his gangster cronies. He is of the underworld, not the netherworld.

Bogart admitted that he had a hard time keeping a straight face while filming *Dr. X*, and his (understandable) lack of conviction in the role is palatable. He leers, though only a little bit, and the look in the eyes is more pitiable than frightening, though that may have just been Bogie feeling sorry for himself. Bogart's Dr. X also looks relatively dapper, for a monster, at least—he has a pince-nez and wears an ascot and classy striped pants that would not be out of place at a formal wedding.

Ads for *The Return of Dr. X* warned "He Lives to Kill . . . And Kills to Live!" and tempted potential patrons with the fear-inspiring tag line, "His unholy power came from steaming test tubes!" The critics looked upon *Dr. X* surprisingly benignly, and some of their comments speak volumes about how greatly the content of movies has changed since 1939: The *New York Post* advised that the film was "guaranteed to give nightmares," while other reviewers called it "a shocker if ever there was one," and adjudged that Bogart's character "may curry moderate favor among the strong of heart. He was just a little too much for us, we admit frankly, and we had no trouble at all with last year's *Frankenstein* and *Dracula* on a double-edged thrill bill."

"It was one of the pictures that made me march in to Jack Warner and ask for more money again," Humphrey Bogart said of *Dr. X* years later. "I was this doctor, brought back to life, and the only thing that nourished the poor bastard was blood. If it had been Jack Warner's blood maybe I wouldn't have minded so much."

Charles Bronson

Death Wish (1974)

"Left-Wing Neanderthal"

*D*eath *Wish* is Charles Bronson's most famous movie and the one that made him, for a while anyway, a mainstream, A-list film star. But consider its premise: A politically liberal New York architect is driven to vigilantism after a savage attack kills his she-had-so-much-to-live-for wife and leaves his daughter catatonic. Think about it. Charles Bronson, a truly primitive screen presence, living on Manhattan's Upper West Side? Voting left-of-center? Charles Bronson as the type of person who might host a cocktail party to raise campaign funds for his representative in Congress—who at the time would have been Bella Abzug? And it turns out that in the Korean War his character was a C.O. No, not a commanding officer, but a *conscientious objector*.

When Bronson has to utter some perfunctory "liberal" dialogue in the beginning of the film (before he has seen the light), his mutterings are so inarticulate that he can hardly be understood. Granted, this is how Charles Bronson always acts, but this time even more so—his distaste for the sentiments is palpable. After a right-wing coworker denigrates him with the clichéd epithet "bleeding-heart liberal," Bronson's response is, "My heart bleeds a little for the underprivileged, yeah." Not for long.

This display of the gentle side of Charles Bronson has just been a prelude to what audiences really paid to see: Bronson offing scum. Given a pistol by a client out West—where men are Men and where New York is referred to as a "toilet"—Bronson uses it when it's his turn to be mugged. There's one final attempt to paint him as Gandhi-esque (he vomits after his first kill), but then he spends the rest of the film baiting criminals and calmly disposing of them. Just like in any other Charles Bronson movie.

Charles Bronson puts his feet up and relaxes after a hard day of slaughtering people.

In the Brian Garfield novel on which *Death Wish* was based, vigilantism was immoral and dangerous and to be avoided at all costs. The movie's lone avenger, on the other hand, is a folk hero—the bad guys come from an assortment of races, colors, and creeds, so that his vendetta couldn't be seen as a racist thing—and an inspired populace similarly takes up arms, with muggings decreasing by fifty percent. The police, handicapped by having to observe those darned old Constitutional rights, are embarrassed that an everyday citizen is responsible for cutting New York's homicide rate, but they also admire the guy's guts.

Because Bronson had often played violent men of action, seeking vengeance is the very thing we expect of him, so his evolution into a Nietzschean Superman carries no emotional weight. (Just the opposite was true of Dustin Hoffman's similar transformation in Sam Peckinpah's *Straw Dogs*: there, because of the actor's cerebral—in the early seventies, at least—persona, the conversion from wimp to mad-dog killer had deep psychological resonance.)

Casting Bronson in *Death Wish* made no sense in terms of the movie's plot and issues. But the filmmakers weren't terribly interested in all that. The supposed thesis of *Death Wish*, that violence had gotten to the point where even a pacifist is provoked into squaring accounts, is just a cynical contrivance to show Charles Bronson on a killing spree. That was even more apparent in the four sequels to the film over the succeeding two decades. Since Bronson's character had now already been established as a murderer, *Death Wish II*, *Death Wish 3*, *Death Wish 4: The Crackdown*, and *Death Wish V: The Face of Death* couldn't pretend to be anything other than mindless bloodfests.

James Caan

For the Boys (1991)

"What's So Funny?"

*C*hronicling fifty years in the life of a singer-comedienne, *For the Boys* had long been Bette Midler's dream project. After forty-one drafts, the script was ready to go. As coproducer, she retained final say regarding casting. She had the female lead, but what about her costar—someone who would be believable as one of those show-business veterans who becomes a national treasure, a song-and-dance man who oozes charisma and pizzazz, even when he's being a reprobate and a schmuck?

Midler had a lot of faith in Mark Rydell, who had directed her in *The Rose*. Still, when he suggested his pal James Caan, an actor who specialized in intense dramatic roles, Midler thought he had to be kidding. "I had cast the role in my mind a hundred times," she recalled. "Mark insisted. I was skeptical. I remembered him from *Godfather* and *Gardens of Stone* and *Misery*. Real tough." Rydell forced her to sit through the Barbra Streisand vehicle, *Funny Lady*. "After I saw that I said, 'Ohhh, I think he'd be great." Then at Rydell's insistence, she became one of the few people who saw his own 1976 movie *Harry and Walter Go to New York*, in which Caan played a con man in old New York. Midler's verdict: "He was hilarious." Caan was in.

There are a number of reasons why *For the Boys* doesn't work as a movie and why it was a monumental flop at the box office: it is a farrago of too many disparate elements (musical, soap-opera saga, comedy, political statement, antiwar tract); the lead characters are unpleasant; its combination of campiness and realism doesn't coalesce; the film is self-reverential. In short, they should have written draft number forty-two. And they should have had a different leading man.

James Caan and Bette Midler are all smiles here, but that was before the box-office grosses on *For the Boys* came in. Actually, the sickly grin on James Caan's face seems to indicate that he knows the news won't be good.

An inveterate United Service Organizations performer, James Caan's character, Eddie Sparks, is reminiscent of Bob Hope (though he was made Jewish so that the resemblance wouldn't be too pronounced), but there are also elements of Sid Caesar, George Burns, George Jessel, and others. Sparks is supposed to be a comic legend; Caan can't deliver a single laugh (and that people watching him within the movie are constantly busting a collective gut only makes his ineffectualness all the more pronounced). Caan seems genuinely nervous. His eyes dart about anxiously, as though he fears somebody's about to tell him it's all a mistake, he's not supposed to be in the film and has to get out. Unlike his agitated eyes, Caan's face often remains immobile, giving him a deer-in-the-headlights look. Prior to the release of *For the Boys*, the press was full of stories about how Caan had frittered away the eighties. (In the *New York Times*, he was said to have "lost almost a decade to drugs and despair.") Unfortunately, the hard times showed in his hardened countenance, and it's not easy to find mirth in someone who has the gray, dispirited look of someone who's seen it all. (The makeup doesn't help matters. Both his pencil mustache and the red tones in his hair are unbecoming—he looks like maybe he might have been a second lead in B pictures at RKO in the forties.)

The Eddie Sparks character and Midler's Dixie Leonard are reputedly a phenomenally successful comedy team, yet the performances of the two actors never mesh. Where he is wan, she is her customary dynamo; the more energy she exudes, the more tired he appears. Midler has an overt love of performing; Caan, frankly, looks miserable to be here. Offstage, Sparks tends to be cretinous, and Caan is somewhat more believable in this guise. Still, there's nothing that suggests the lady killer Sparks is purported to be, and Caan lacks the facile charm you need if you're going to get away with being as ill-natured and self-involved as this character is. Caan is completely convincing in only one scene. During the Vietnam sequence, a jaded army audience pushes him to the background so they can get closer to a go-go girl onstage. In this moment Sparks is panicked at having lost control and being out of his element, just as Caan is throughout the film. For a brief moment actor and character have become one.

If James Caan read his reviews, he saw that he was "burned-out," "charmless," "generally uncomfortable," and "wretchedly miscast." Yet he refused to shoulder any responsibility for the failure of *For the Boys*. During a press junket for his next film, *Honeymoon in Vegas*, Caan was asked his opinion on why the highly anticipated Midler vehicle had tanked. "Bette Midler is very stupid," he was quoted as saying. "She's not a bad person, but stupid in terms of gray matter. I mean I like her, but I like my dog, too." A year later he raged to *Movieline*:

> I'll go to my grave saying that there was a great movie in *For the Boys*. We shot it and Mark [Rydell], the editor, and I know it. The pain Mark went through on that. It was [20th Century–Fox head] Barry Diller, Mark was just overpowered. Literally every day, I'd say, 'Mark, you've got a contract. You've got plenty of clout. There is such a great movie there. Just play the fucking story. And tell him to get the fuck out of there.' It's not a Bette Midler fucking, motherfucking musical. It's not for the fucking fruits in the bathhouse and the old ladies in New York. It's a story about people. A great, great, great movie was destroyed.

Midler was devastated by the fate of *For the Boys*. (And as though the film's box-office failure wasn't bad enough, Midler found herself being sued—unsuccessfully as it turned out—by Martha Raye. The Big Mouth, a U.S.O. veteran, claimed that *For The Boys* had appropriated her life story.) Midler remained diplomatic about the movie but eventually suggested to a talk-show host that Caan could have been "a little funnier." One assumes that after this experience, Bette learned to trust her own instincts.

Tom Hanks and Bruce Willis

The Bonfire of the Vanities (1990)

"Nice Guy Finishes Last (And So Does Bruce Willis)"

The *Bonfire of the Vanities* was a complete debacle, and the irreversible seeds of disaster were planted very early on. As soon as the key casting decisions were made, this movie was doomed.

Tom Wolfe's monumentally misanthropic novel is a quintessential document of New York City in the Reagan/Koch years. A keenly observed social satire, *The Bonfire of the Vanities* finds the venality lurking within the heart of every New Yorker, no matter what his or her domain. What particularly distinguishes Wolfe's writing is his pinpoint accuracy in dissecting Gotham from the upper reaches of Park Avenue society to the lower depths of the inner city. The novel is so effective because Wolfe exaggerates only to the slightest degree: he didn't need to do anything more. It had the makings of a terrific movie.

Self-defined as a Master of the Universe, the filthy rich bond trader Sherman McCoy is described by Wolfe as "tall . . . almost six-one . . . terrific posture . . . terrific to the point of imperious." In a world of Us and Them, he is one of Them. His are people of heft—not fat, but a heft that comes from their own sense of self-importance, as well as from too many meals at the Four Seasons and too many glasses of Chivas. Heft is something Tom Hanks does not have. An easygoing, self-effacing actor with a puppyish demeanor, he is one of Us (which accounts for his popularity in the first place). There is nothing formidable in Hanks's screen presence; rather than a go-for-the-jugular killer bond trader from Old Stock, he's a hustling mid-level Yuppie. Never mind not being a Master of the Universe, Hanks isn't even master of his own home. He's dwarfed by the enormity of his own apartment. Hanks was thirty-three when he filmed

Bonfire and looked several years younger; Sherman McCoy is thirty-eight, but his overbearing manner would have made him appear older. (As wrong as Hanks is for this part, he was not as illogical as the first actor Warner Bros. had considered: Tom Cruise.)

Sherman McCoy is arrogance personified; Hanks can be sardonic but he registers decency too strongly to emit pure, utter contempt. McCoy is unflappable, but, from the outset, when he mistakenly dials his wife rather than his girlfriend, Hanks verges on the apoplectic. As the world crashes down on Tom Hanks's Sherman McCoy, he seems pathetic: you don't have the satisfaction of seeing an s.o.b. getting his comeuppance. (Coproducer Peter Guber had first hit upon the idea of Hanks exactly because Sherman McCoy was so unsympathetic. His reasoning was that you need a lovable actor to play such an unlikable character. The obvious question then is why bother adapting the book at all?) William Hurt was the actor most frequently cited when people imagined themselves the casting director for *The Bonfire of the Vanities*. Hurt would have damaged the film in his own special way—his droning presence would have embalmed the material. The ideal actor would have been John Heard, who wasn't a big enough name for an "important project" like this.

The choice of Bruce Willis to play journalist Peter Fallow was equally infelicitous. Fallow is an alcoholic British reporter for a sleazy tabloid newspaper; Willis doesn't try to be British. It's too bad because not only does the Englishness of the character provide a sense of accuracy—his newspaper is clearly modeled on the *New York Post*, whose owner Rupert Murdoch imported many Brits—but it also works thematically, because Fallow becomes the jaded outsider who keeps an eye on what's happening in the colonies. Think John Hurt in the role or, going younger, Gary Oldman. Warners people felt that John Cleese would make an excellent Fallow, and they were right, but the star of *A Fish Called Wanda* was otherwise engaged.

Director Brian De Palma got to thinking that since Fallow would be narrating the movie, audiences would probably prefer to hear an American voice. When Bruce Willis got wind of Fallow's change of citizenship, he let it be known that he might be available. Certainly De Palma could have found a more capable actor than Willis—all he had to do was walk into a Manhattan or L.A. restaurant and he'd have seen any number waiting tables. It's funny that in his action films, where he's posturing as a

They look so unsuspecting. But soon after this publicity photo for
The Bonfire of the Vanities was taken, Tom Hanks and Bruce Willis
would find themselves in one of the all-time Hollywood bombs.

hero, Willis has always seemed faintly sleazy and smarmy. Now he's called
upon to impart those very qualities and he's incapable. Willis is not even
a convincing drunk, and the effect of having his inexpressive voice-over
dominate the film is benumbing. He's a hopeless narrator, one who gets
tongue-tied over a sentence that contains the words "inexplicably" and
"inextricably." And when he gets to the more "literary" passages, watch
out. Who would have imagined that the line, "He followed her through
the room, past the grinning faces full of boiling teeth, past the conversa-
tional bouquets, past the impeccably emaciated ladies of society, the social
X rays," could be rendered utterly devoid of malice or irony?

Much of the supporting cast gives the impression either of having been chosen as names out of a hat or of being simply misdirected. Melanie Griffith is much fleshier and déclassé than Wolfe's rendering of McCoy's mistress, Maria Ruskin, and Kim Cattrell lacks the icy refinement of his wife, Judy. (De Palma and writer Michael Cristoffer turn both women into ditzes). The single loopiest casting decision was in regard to the man presiding over McCoy's trial, Judge Kovitsky, who may be splenetic but is also the most decent person in Wolfe's universe. Alan Arkin had been signed to play the jurist, but the Warners brass got antsy. They realized the movie had no sympathetic black characters, plus there was something about having a Jewish judge dismiss a case against a white defendant in a racially charged trial. So they dropped Arkin and replaced him with Morgan Freeman, who gave a closing speech about justice in which he admonishes unruly court spectators that "Decency is what your grand-mother taught you." If you have to listen to lines like this, though, you might as well hear them in Freeman's exquisite voice.

Had *The Bonfire of the Vanities* been perfectly cast, it still would have failed. Through his misguided approach, Brian De Palma tells the story in excessively broad strokes and thereby loses the anthropological qual-ity of the material. The social satire has become a cartoon.

Diane Keaton

The Little Drummer Girl (1984)

"Annie Get Your Gun"

When Diane Keaton was announced for the film version of John LeCarré's book about a pro-Palestinian actress recruited by the Israeli secret service, the jokes were immediate in coming. *Time* ran a squib about Keaton's learning to use a bazooka and assault rifle for the movie and quoted her as saying, "I never did anything like that before. But I loved it." The magazine then suggested, "How about a sequel called *Annie Hall Goes to War?*"

Curiously, what's wrong much of the time with Keaton's presence in *The Little Drummer Girl* is that she's too far-removed from her former comic persona. In the book, the lead character, who is English, was widely thought to be modeled after Vanessa Redgrave, but author LeCarré said Keaton's Charlie was based on his half-sister, an actress with the Royal Shakespeare Company. The movie's Charlie does live in London, but now she originally comes from Iowa. On the printed page, the character is in her early twenties and thus impressionable enough for her beliefs, which she had supposed were deeply held, to be manipulated. Keaton was in her late thirties when she made the film. One assumes that at this age a person's political convictions, although not completely intractable, are firmly enough entrenched so that it would take an excessive amount of inculcation to change them.

Keaton's initial line of dialogue in *The Little Drummer Girl* is, "The Palestinians have been *robbed!* They've been driven off of land that's been theirs for centuries and now they're herded off into camps!" First impressions being what they are, it's only natural that we assume her militant pro-Palestinian stance to be her dominant character trait. Thus, it comes

Diane Keaton has apparently forsaken the thrift shops of her Annie Hall days for army-navy surplus stores.

as a surprise that all it takes is a couple of hours with the Israeli secret agents who have kidnapped her for Charlie to evince an interest in helping them track down a bigwig Palestinian terrorist. She does put up a little bit of defiance ("Why don't you leave the poor fucking Arabs alone? Why don't you give them back the land you stole from them?"), but once she gets some soulful looks from Yorgo Voyagis, as the agent who abducted her, she's in.

This quick change might have been more believable if Keaton was portraying the character in the dizzy style of her Woody Allen days. (In the book, Charlie *is* of the dithery Annie Hall school.) But when she made *The Little Drummer Girl* Keaton had her performances in *Reds* and *Shoot the Moon* under her belt and, by general consensus, was now an accomplished dramatic actress. A serious Charlie, however, doesn't lend credibility to a film which, because of its all-around implausibility, needs all it can get. In addition, the intricate series of chicaneries that lead to her espionage work in the first place (involving stolen diaries and the Israelis' working knowledge of her life history) don't seem to confound her in the least. Keaton retains her equanimity, which is odd considering that we in the audience are certainly discombobulated by events, and she's the one who's in the center of them.

But Keaton can't completely escape the pixilated image of her past. It may be unfair, but the phrase "la-dee-dah" will always be associated with her in our minds. Thus, in the scenes in which she's at her most determinedly serious—wearing army fatigues and doing calisthenics with a rifle at a Palestinian training base, planting a bomb with a calculated air of nonchalance—she's funny because she looks so incongruous, the same way that Goldie Hawn was funny going through boot camp in *Private Benjamin.* There *are* moments when she's carrying out acts of espionage and falls back on some of her comic mannerisms, and when she has trouble parking a car in which she's delivering explosives, one can't help but think of Woody Allen's inability to parallel park in *Annie Hall.*

The Little Drummer Girl is thoroughly unnecessary, a movie that seems to exist only because there was a bestselling book first. When it's over, all it adds up to is a cursory trip through England, Greece, West Germany, Lebanon, Israel, and points in between. And then you realize that two hours of your life that you will never have back again were spent watching a bunch of secret agents doing little more than engaging in surveillance.

Michael Keaton

Batman (1989)

"Not Your Father's Superhero"

How did it come to pass that the unprepossessing, slightly anemic, five-foot-ten Michael Keaton impersonated Batman? This is what happens when Hollywood money men try to be creative. Producers Jon Peters and Peter Guber were looking to revamp—after fifty years—the image of the legendary comic-book superhero. Peters said their objective was to cast an actor who "wasn't the *conventional* choice, you know, the perfect Superman-type person," so that audiences would be treated to "a new form of hero, a more realistic hero than what we've been seeing."

Peters and Guber had originally thought of Bill Murray, a performer whose stance of ironic detachment could be useful in putting a revisionist spin on a pop icon who had been portrayed with straightforward steadfastness in serials back in the forties and with an appealing blank-faced campiness by Adam West on TV in the mid-sixties. Murray didn't pan out, though, and other actors considered for the role encompassed the orthodox (Pierce Brosnan), the vacuous (Charlie Sheen), and the just plain bad (the wooden Mel Gibson who, with those stubby little legs of his, would have looked absurd in the Batman costume).

Warner Bros. production chief Mark Canton was in sync with the Peters-Guber view of a newfangled Batman/Bruce Wayne: "I decided it would be better not to have a square-jawed guy. . . . You needed someone more complex and more accessible. Someone you could relate to in street clothes." Although Michael Keaton hadn't worn street clothes as the insufferable gremlin in *Beetlejuice*, Jon Peters said that when Canton, Guber, and he saw the film, "we went 'Wow!' Michael is so explosive in that character, almost *dangerous*."

Nerd millionaire by day, nerd superhero by night. In contrast to Michael Keaton, however, Michael Gough exudes class as Alfred.

When the announcement was made that the improbable Michael Keaton was going to star as the Caped Crusader, tens of thousands of Batman buffs mobilized. Feeling a bitter sense of betrayal, they put down their dog-eared copies of *Detective Comics* long enough to draw up petitions and organize letter-writing campaigns demanding that this heart-sickening decision be reversed. The New York *Daily News* paraphrased their concerns: "Batman is not a wimp, they cried. Batman is not a clown, they begged. Batman is not a softie, they said." One distraught fellow vented in a letter to the *Los Angeles Times* that "Warner Bros. and Burton have defecated on the history of Batman." Keaton rolled his eyes about the controversy he had engendered. "I didn't realize it could be such an issue," he admitted. "I mean we're talking about Batman. Grow up!"

Director Tim Burton defended his leading man: "I had trouble finding any weight in the fact [Bruce Wayne] is so handsome and so rich—what the hell does he have to go and put on a Batsuit for? With Michael it seemed to make a lot of sense." As things ended up, Keaton's participation in *Batman* made as little sense as the protestors had feared, although not for the reasons they had anticipated. Keaton did not turn their hero into a joke; he refrained from his manic Beetlejuice riffs and his gonzo routine from *Night Shift*. The most noteworthy thing about

Keaton's presence in *Batman* is his lack of presence. He's a lump, a leaden figure. For all the producers' talk of a new kind of Batman, Keaton doesn't redefine Bruce Wayne and his mysterious alter ego as much as he reduces them.

Tim Burton set out to present a neurotic Bruce Wayne, a man whose anxieties stem from seeing his parents murdered as a young boy. Keaton is not actor enough to impart this inner turmoil: being sluggish is not the same as being tormented. Wayne is also fabulously rich, but with his light voice and offhanded manner, the weaselly Keaton lacks the refinement and physical authority that presumably would accompany his character's rank. Michael Gough as Wayne's butler, Alfred, is the one who reeks of class.

Keaton's lack of stature not only hobbles his impersonation of Bruce Wayne but also renders him rather pathetic once he puts on his costume. An actor playing Batman doesn't necessarily have to have a classic strong profile, but he should at least *have* a profile. Keaton's weak chin, pursed mouth, and stingy nose can't stand up to the Batmask. He's playing a crime fighter who utilizes not superpowers, but agility and stealthiness, yet Keaton is devoid of gracefulness: he's an action hero as clodhopper. Although supposedly filled with righteous indignation, the most that Keaton can muster when he's going after despicable thugs is half a sneer—he looks mildly discomfited. The hebetudinous actor is overpowered by the massive, attention-grabbing Gotham City production design and by Jack Nicholson's mad performance as the Joker. Keaton becomes an extra in his own movie. If Peters, Guber, Canton, and Burton truly wanted a different kind of Batman, they should have at least chosen someone strong enough to counterbalance all the rigmarole in the movie. I wonder if Gilbert Gottfried was available.

Even though it's not much fun, *Batman* became, of course, a phenomenal box-office success, thanks to a monumental marketing push. It used to be said that movies were all about the art of the deal. *Batman* signaled that now it's the art of the publicity machine.

Mary Tyler Moore and Elvis Presley

Change of Habit (1969)

"In the Ghetto"

Elvis had grown tired of all those mindless movies in which, after some inevitable romantic misunderstandings and forgettable pop songs, he ended up in a clinch with Nancy Sinatra or Shelley Fabares. Already in 1969 he had appeared in the Western *Charro!* and now he was trying to get relevant, baby. Wanted to comment on where it's at, on what's happenin'. Sad to say, in 1969, Elvis simply wasn't hip (the King hadn't been considered cool since about 1963). Equally regrettable—if not surprising—is that *Change of Habit* has the feel of a counterculture movie as it might have been envisioned by someone in the Nixon administration. It's what, at the time, would have been called "plastic."

Everything about the character Presley plays is wrong for him. First of all, he's a doctor. Try to envision an Elvis who had studied organic chemistry and learned to cut up cadavers; picture him taking the MCATs and surviving an internship. Second, he runs a health clinic in a black and Puerto Rican neighborhood in a generic city. One way he wins the hearts and minds of the locals is through his music. Not salsa, or rhythm-and-blues, or soul, not even good rock 'n' roll like he used to sing in the old days. No, he plays bubble gum music, and the inner-city folks are groovin' to it. If you were in a generous mood, you might force yourself to accept Presley heading a clinic in Appalachia, but there's no way that he'd make it in the Big Town.

Elvis was never an actor but he always—even here—had a distinctive screen presence. That's not necessarily a good thing, because whether he's treating an old lady who's suffered a heart attack or curing a little girl of autism *in one session*, he employs the same patented bad-boy swagger

If Elvis is somewhat dour, it's only because he just recently found out that the nurse he had the hots for is really a nun. If Mary Tyler Moore looks a bit out of sorts, it's that bad habit, which is hardly flattering. (Museum of Modern Art/Film Stills Archives)

that goes back to *Love Me Tender*. He'd clearly prefer to be raising a ruckus or scarfing down a heaping one of his favorite junk food concoctions like Pepsi Jell-O with marshmallows than making house calls. This does not make for a reassuring bedside manner.

Dr. Presley is aided by three nuns. Mary Tyler Moore is their leader. She wasn't regarded as cool in 1969 either. Earlier in the decade Moore had seemed like the greatest young American wife imaginable: sexy, funny, smart, and a perfect companion. But the goodwill engendered by *The Dick Van Dyke Show* had been frittered away when Moore tried to become a movie star and appeared in two pathetic comedies, the quality of which can be gleaned from their titles: *Don't Just Stand There* and *What's So Bad About Feeling Good?*

For the few people who saw *Change of Habit* when it was released, the problem was reconciling the Laura Petrie of *The Dick Van Dyke Show*—who, it was understood, was a sexually fulfilled woman—with a nun, even one as progressive as Sister Michelle. Moore is a light actress who relies more on a winning personality and adept comic timing than any particular dramatic skills. In this film, her most salient trait is coquettishness, which is not a quality a nun is going to be able to put to much use. Moore possesses neither the serene piousness of a woman who would have joined a convent in the first place nor the zealousness of the social activist Sister Michelle is.

Watching this movie today, all you can see is Mary Richards from *The Mary Tyler Moore Show*, for her voice and demeanor are exactly the same as when she was at WJM-TV in Minneapolis. (The series began shooting several months after this film.) Plus, due to the demands of the plot—"If we're gonna reach these people, we've to be accepted first as

This time, Elvis is in uniform, Mary Tyler Moore (and fellow nun, Barbara McNair) out.

women, then as nuns," she explains—Moore spends most of the film in civilian dress, the same ugly clothing of the period that Mary Richards wore. (During the opening credits, the three sisters are stripping off their habits. It looks like a scene from a particularly kinky movie for a very specialized audience.) The habit was unusually unbecoming to Moore because the headpiece covered her cheeks, leaving little room on her face for anything other than her very generous mouth.

The people involved in it may have kidded themselves they were dealing with the searing issues of the era, but *Change of Habit* is so simplistic that its slum neighborhood is as well scrubbed as Bing Crosby's city parish in *Going My Way* twenty-five years earlier. Despite the inclusion of dialogue on the order of "You're locked in with those ofay chicks," and "Would you diagnose what's happening today—the riots, the student unrest—as not really the death throes of an old order but the birth pangs of a new one?" and even with Sister Michelle's crisis of faith as she contemplates leaving the convent to marry her doctor, *Change of Habit* is just another feckless vehicle for Elvis, no deeper than *Harum Scarum*. The film's sole interest is in seeing the king of rock 'n' roll, in his last film, and America's Sweetheart of the 1970s side by side, two icons whom you wouldn't even have expected to see in the same room.

Bill Murray

The Razor's Edge (1984)

"Magical Mystery Tour"

When it was released in 1984, *Ghostbusters* became the highest grossing comedy to that time. Had it not been for the long-dead British novelist W. Somerset Maugham, however, the spectral special-effects comedy would never have been made.

Maugham's *The Razor's Edge* is about as persuasive as a novel from the dubious Searching-for-the-Meaning-of-Life genre can be. (It certainly beats *Jonathan Livingston Seagull*.) The book must have meant a lot to Bill Murray. He held Columbia Pictures hostage before agreeing to replace the deceased John Belushi in *Ghostbusters*. The terms of the ransom were that he would get slimed only if the studio agreed to bankroll his dream project, a new version of the Maugham novel.

It's curious that after having forced Columbia's hand, Murray seemed so apathetic about the movie. As Maugham's peregrine, Larry Darrell, an insouciant young man from Lake Forrest, Illinois, who turns serious after getting a gander at a lot of corpses as an ambulance driver in the Great War, Murray scarcely gave a performance at all. Larry came back from Over There in one piece only because someone else took a bayonet thrust that was intended for him. As a result (although the year is 1918 and the character was created by Maugham in 1944), Murray's Larry does a put-down of eighties Yuppie values: "I got a second chance at life and I am not going to waste it on a big house, a new car every year, and a bunch of friends who want a big house and a new car every year." He post-pones his wedding, telling his fiancée, Isabel, "I'm not happy. I can't make myself happy. I couldn't make you happy. I just have to think. I need to think. And I don't have much experience in that field." To which Cather-

ine Hicks's Isabel, sounding like a volun-
teer in Ronald Reagan's 1984 reelection
campaign, replies, "Think? Think about
what?"

By this point, Murray's presence in
this movie is already problematic. He's a
performer whose stock-in-trade is irony.
The smirk that's always threatening to
form on the sides of his mouth, the leering look on his face, the ever-present hint
of contempt in his voice—these are his
signals that we shouldn't take anything
about him too seriously. But his well-
established image catches up to him in
The Razor's Edge: whenever Larry Darrell is being solemn and passionately dis-
coursing upon heartfelt ideas, it's a no go.
You're so accustomed to Murray's dry
causticity that when he speaks about
needing to find inner peace, you feel like
it's part of a gag. Murray seems already

No, it's not a sketch from *Saturday Night
Live*; Bill Murray is trying to be serious as
he contemplates the meaning of life up in the
Himalayas.

to have figured out what life's all about—it's one big joke.

In the 1946 version of *The Razor's Edge*, Tyrone Power was bland but
certainly sincere; the emotional restlessness of Power's Larry may have
been nebulous, but he made it clear that *something* was spooking him.
Here, you're aware that Bill Murray's character has been deeply affected
by what he witnessed in the war only because he sometimes stares off
into space.

Larry Darrell apparently can't do his metaphysical journey of the soul
in the confines of Lake Forrest, or even Chicago, so it's off to Paris. Does
Larry take advantage of his privileged background and stay at the Ritz,
contemplate works of art at the Louvre, spend hours jawing with great
thinkers at the Sorbonne, and hang out at cafes with other members of
the Lost Generation comparing existential notes while downing large
quantities of absinthe? Nah. He lives in a cramped dump in a outré part
of town and tries to learn the meaning of life working as a fish packer in
Les Halles. Apparently that doesn't work because the next thing we know

he's off digging in a coal mine somewhere. Then, after a fellow miner turns him on to how cool Indian mysticism is, Larry heads off to the Himalayas, where he engages in typically goofy Bill Murray–type shenanigans with the locals. After confabbing with a Holy Man, he sits on a snow-capped mountain reading books. He trembles a bit and burns some of the books and then voilà! He comes down from the mountain. Enlightenment is his.

What exactly has transpired in his head remains a mystery, because the only thing he clues us in on is this bit of wisdom: "It is easy to be a Holy Man on the top of a mountain." Up to now, the main problem with Murray in this role was the baggage of his career: it was impossible to take him seriously in his quest for knowledge. But now, his limitations as an actor do him in. Post-epiphany, he's still the same Bill Murray: still deadpan, still flippant, still teetering on the sarcastic.

Anyway, Larry's ready to save the world, while once again working in the stalls at the Paris marketplace. In another example of 1980s sensibility thrown into a period piece, he cures a pal of chronic headaches with a stone he picked up in India—remember crystals? Larry's main mission, though, is to redeem an old friend, Sophie (Theresa Russell), who has become a drunken, drug-addicted slut in Paris, all because her husband and kid died. He tries to convince her that dope is for dopes (largely by doing more Bill Murray things, like imitating an Indian and sitting in wet paint). Ultimately, though, he's unsuccessful, as Sophie ends up in the Seine with her throat slit. Larry then goes off to do more good deeds with his newfound wisdom. The End. In short, material that in Somerset Maugham's novel was, if not exactly profound, at least thoughtful, has been rendered awfully silly.

It really was too bad that all those people who had enjoyed *Ghostbusters* didn't come out for *The Razor's Edge* a few months later: Even though he's grappling with Big Ideas instead of the Stay-Puff man, Bill Murray gives essentially the same performance.

Sharon Stone

Intersection (1994)

"Not Tonight, Dear, I Have a Headache"

Sharon Stone became a major star by exposing a voracious sexuality on screen. Having once uncrossed her legs to show the world she wasn't wearing panties, she might have been expecting too much in asking audiences to accept her as a frigid old thing.

In *Intersection*, Richard Gere—who is about to have a serious car accident and maybe die—sees parts of his life flash before his eyes, in particular, his relationships with two women. He has had to choose between trying to rekindle the spark for his spouse, Sharon Stone, or starting a new life with his girlfriend, Lolita Davidovitch. The love has gone out of his marriage—why is not clear, although it wouldn't be a day at the beach living with the gloomy, self-centered jerk Gere plays. *Intersection* is a languid little movie featuring people whose problems are not in the least bit interesting.

The wife is intended to seem cold, self-involved, and standoffish to her husband's affections. In an attempt to undermine expectations of how anyone portrayed by Sharon Stone would behave in a movie, the actress is costumed in tailored suits, classic upper-class fashion that screams "unapproachable." Her hair is in a bun, perhaps, like the coif of Bebe Neuwirth's Lilith on *Cheers*, a visual pun for how tightly wound and repressed this woman is. Though, come on, this is Sharon Stone, so how uptight could she possibly look?

In movies such as *Basic Instinct* and *Total Recall*, squalid as they may have been, Stone had a vivaciousness that was tremendously appealing. Here, it is Lolita Davidovitch who, as Gere's blowsy lover, gets to be extroverted and impassioned. In contrast to Davidovitch's dynamism,

Taking a different tack than usual, Sharon Stone covers up her body with a table.

Stone is demure, ponderous, and ramrod straight. Futilely attempting to appear brittle, she speaks softly and crisply and lowers her eyes a lot. As written, her character is an Ice Queen, a prim woman who no longer has any interest in physical intimacy. But, hey, we're not stupid. We know what Sharon Stone is capable of, so we have to assume that she is playing a coy game of seduction, as if challenging Gere's character to be enough of a man to pique her interest. (The film is foolish enough to give us a glimpse of the Sharon Stone we know and admire: a flashback shows her and Gere's first anniversary party, back when they were still filled with lust for each other. Fully clothed, she mounts the reclining Gere for a quick coital interlude in the library while their guests are in another room.)

Director Mark Rydell said that in her fervor to play a different type of role, Stone "pursued this part so avidly, she was like a schnauzer on my pant leg." The ultimate effect of Stone's casting in *Intersection*, however, is just the opposite of what was intended: it seems that the woman must be dying to burst out of the confines of her Junior League wardrobe, let her hair down, and get some action going.

Patrick Swayze

City of Joy (1992)

"Prognosis: Hopeless"

Has there ever been as inexpressive an actor as Patrick Swayze—or at least such an actor who has gained some modicum of success? Admittedly, Swayze does little harm to mindless action films like *Road House*, where the characters are two-dimensional and the stakes aren't too great anyway. But when you're making an "important motion picture," this is not the person you want for the lead.

If Swayze can't be accused of ruining *City of Joy*, it's only because director Roland Joffe and the dreadful writer Mark Medoff had already done so. This is one of those movies in which downtrodden people suffer so that a sensitive middle-class white person can get his head screwed back on straight. In this case, Swayze is a Houston doctor who chucks it all away after a young girl dies on his operating table. (His explanation of his status: "You've got your nonpracticing Catholics, I'm a nonpracticing doctor.") He goes to India "to find enlightenment" but gets stranded in Calcutta after misplacing his passport ("Oh, Goddamn, I must have left it at the ashram") and losing his money in a mugging.

The robbery lands the injured Dr. Max in the titular health clinic. Though he fights the urge, you haven't seen many movies if you don't immediately realize that he'll become the hardest-working doctor the place has ever seen. He also is the Great White Father, teaching the poverty-stricken Indians how important self-respect and self-reliance are and egging them on to stand up to the oppression of the local godfather. As the silver-tongued Dr. Max puts it, "I am telling you, if you don't stop this asshole now, he will rule you for the rest of your lives!"

You wouldn't know it from the goofy smile on his face, but Patrick Swayze is experiencing a crisis of faith in *City of Joy*.

That Patrick Swayze has had any career at all can only be explained by the sole quality he is capable of putting across on screen—sincerity. He's so sincere, in fact, that it can get embarrassing, but apparently it's this unaffectedness that appeals to the girls and young women who make up his constituency. Swayze's shallow earnestness makes no sense in the context of *City of Joy*, however, for it runs counter to the dark cynicism with which Dr. Max is supposedly consumed. Contrary to manifesting a nihilistic attitude toward the world, Swayze seems more like a nice young man who's being a wee bit peevish today because he locked his keys in the car.

Swayze is hopeless. As usual, his line readings are given in a drone, his tendency is to mumble, and his little eyes are deadened and fishlike. When he wants to show an emotion, whether it's concern, rage, or guilt, he furrows his brow and scrunches up his face. He seems convinced that by adding wrinkles to his visage he looks wizened and is therefore imbuing himself with an aura of gravity. The movie's most hilarious moment comes at the end when, having found that elusive enlightenment he's been after, Swayze tells Pauline Collins, who runs the clinic, "I bet you never expected me to say I'm glad to be here," explaining, "I never felt more alive." Which he says in his most lifeless monotone.

At first Roland Joffe had been leaning toward casting Warren Beatty or Richard Dreyfuss in *City of Joy*, but Swayze buttonholed him and, crying real tears, talked some sense out of the director, arguing that if the character was played by an older actor he would be "boring." Swayze's logic was, "I felt the only way for people to care about this guy is he had to be in a youthful rage of rebelling in any way that he can. He's like an unleashed cyclone." A zephyr, actually.

Shortly before *City of Joy* opened, Swayze said, "I had come to a place where my insides were screaming . . . I am a movie star and am given the opportunity to make a lot of movies. I couldn't feel why I was empty inside. *City of Joy* came along and I realized why. I was screaming for a movie that would help me find what the next level as an actor was and then to see if I had the ability to achieve it." He didn't.

CITY SLICKERS

A trio of actors who did not look at home on the range

Normally for James Cagney, "way out west" would mean Riverside Drive, but here he is having a high old time on the Cherokee Strip.

James Cagney

The Oklahoma Kid (1939)

"I'm in a New York State of Mind"

James Cagney: By definition, the quintessential New York actor. It was the scrappy Cagney who, more than anyone else, epitomized the vitality, the brashness, the sheer energy of the place, the Get-Outta-My-Way attitude that sometimes frightens the tourists dawdling on midtown sidewalks. The city is always in motion and so, on-screen, was Cagney.

James Cagney in a Western. You might as well drop Hell's Kitchen into the middle of Monument Valley. The mix is wrong. In the beginning of *The Oklahoma Kid* there's Cagney on a horse. He's stealing government money that the Bad Guys had stolen while it was being delivered to the Cherokees as reparation for grabbing the Oklahoma Territory away from them. Cagney has a smile on his face. He knows he doesn't belong here and so do we. Suddenly we get it. This is how Warner Bros.—the studio that had staked out its claim as Hollywood's voice of working class urbanites—was dealing with the late thirties craze for big-budget Westerns: It provided for all the expensive trappings but everything else was to be purposely fatuous. Look! Gangster Humphrey Bogart is on hand, too, dressed all in black, wreaking havoc and going by the name of Whip McCord. His presence is also a pretty good joke. (In Cagney's previous film, *Angels With Dirty Faces*, Cagney and Bogart were in their element as New York racketeers.)

The movie is only a few minutes' old when Cagney goes into a saloon, and, instead of busting up the place like an outlaw in any other Western would have done, he reverts to his roots as a Broadway song-and-dance man: he stands by the piano and sings "I Don't Want to Play in Your Yard." And when members of Bogart's gang try to cause trouble, Cagney keeps on trilling even as he punches out Ward Bond and draws his pistol. Cockamamie stuff.

So you settle in, enjoying how Cagney has not altered his staccato delivery or even attempted a drawl. *Time* declared that his "Bowery accent lends an admirably exotic touch to his impersonation of a badlands sharp-shooter." Suddenly, though, he explains why he doesn't put much stock in "civilization" and why he's not swept up in the empire-building that's sweeping the country. "I don't take to this itch for plowing up new empires," he tells a disbelieving Donald Crisp. Any why not? Because "the white people steal the land from the Indians." When Crisp protests that they are paid for the land, Cagney answers, "A measly dollar and forty cents an acre. Price agreed to at the point of a gun. Then the immigrants sweat and strain and break their hearts carving out a civilization. Fine. Great. And when they get it all pretty and prosperous, along come the grafters and land-grabbers and politicians. And with one hand skim off the cream and with the other scoop up the gravy." All of a sudden, *The Oklahoma Kid* is sounding like one of the liberal social dramas at which Warners excelled. It's become something serious.

This sobriety becomes even more pronounced when Cagney's father, the mayor of Tulsa—yes, this movie's plot is convoluted—is arrested on phony charges and Bogart organizes a vigilante group. The kindly and upright mayor is lynched. The sight of the rope blowing in the wind after the deed has been completed is most unsettling, especially since things started off so lightheartedly. Now we're really in deep with the weightiness, as the movie transforms into an antivigilante discourse. And Cagney's presence, which had originally seemed so charming, becomes distressingly inapt. He and Bogart are like a couple of kids playing cowboy, and the effect is not unlike a civil rights drama enacted by whites in blackface. You wish that, in making a film about an important subject that in the thirties was so timely, the studio had cast an actor from its contract roster who could be taken seriously in those circumstances, even if that person were as bland a presence as Ronald Reagan.

Jack Lemmon

Cowboy (1958)

"Saddle Sore"

J ack Lemmon starring in a Western is a logical enough concept. Bob Hope, Laurel and Hardy, the Marx Brothers, Red Skelton, and countless others had all starred in cowboy spoofs, so why not Lemmon, who in 1958 was the leading young light comedian in Hollywood. The only problem was that *Cowboy* was not a comedy. It was the real thing. Or at least it tried to be.

Lemmon plays a callow Chicago hotel desk clerk who wants to be a cowboy in the worst way. Glenn Ford is a legendary cattle herder (what a strange concept) who, having blown his money gambling, grudgingly accepts Lemmon as a partner and takes him along on a roundup. We know that Ford's character is colorful because, even though he's a macho outdoorsman, he loves the opera, and when he's sitting in his hotel bathtub he shoots cockroaches on the wall. That's it for intentional humor in this film.

Directed by Delmer Daves, whose crowning achievements—the über-camp family melodramas *A Summer Place* and *Susan Slade*—were just around the corner, *Cowboy* was promoted as an "adult" Western. This did not mean that bawdy saloon girls showed off their gams and then some, but that the film self-consciously eschewed cattle rustlers, gunfights, and Indian raids (although there are a few Comanches hovering about in one scene) to concentrate on character development along the trail.

The movie could have used gunslingers for this is very dull stuff. Although *Cowboy* avoids some clichés, it dishes up a whole other set of banalities as it galumphs along the expected route. Anything you'd anticipate befalling Lemmon's city slicker does indeed happen. Starting out,

Jack Lemmon, a product of prep schools and Harvard, gets pointers on roughing it from Brian Donlevy, who spent *his* teens battling Pancho Villa and fighting in World War I.

Lemmon is given the wildest, most unrestrained horse to fall off of, much to the amusement of the veterans. He even has to be taught how to put on chaps. This tenderfoot feels repulsed by the callous indifference of his cohorts when one of the gang is threatened or dies, and is appalled by their single-minded fixation on delivering the herd of cattle. Flinty Glenn Ford treats Jack harshly, almost sadistically, but—dontchaknow?—that's because he's awfully fond of the younger man and wants him to be able to handle whatever life throws at him. Toughen him he does, and Lemmon becomes the meanest, most hardhearted varmint in the bunch. That's the idea, anyway.

Not an actor who fits comfortably into a period film, Lemmon isn't very convincing at any of this. After only four years of making movies, he had already established himself as a quintessential male of the American mid-century, a brash go-getter. He would perfect this persona a little later, notably in *The Apartment*, but these very contemporary qualities were already well rooted. His screen presence is too knowing, too self-aware, too calculating to make him a convincing greenhorn in the early scenes. You could believe Lemmon scheming to *get out of* this cattle trail—although that would make *Cowboy* a comedy—but no way would he be eager to rough it. (In real life, the actor was petrified of horses and, according to Glenn Ford, only agreed to do the film after Ford got him liquored up and cast aspersions on his manhood. An inebriated Lemmon wasn't going to stand for that, and he signed for the role.)

Lemmon is even less persuasive in the latter part of the film, when he has become truculent and unfeeling. In his previous movies, Lemmon had played mischievous roués, likable young men scheming to get the girl or some other object of his affection. His modus operandi had been his charm. Here when he's itching for a fight and being confrontational, or bawling orders to the other men on the cattle run, he's not in the least bit intimidating. It's akin to a dweebish college student who, after being bullied for three years, is at long last a senior and is determined to give the freshman pledges a hard time. His sneer is comical and not unlike the expression he would later use in playing the outrageously cartoonish villain in 1965's *The Great Race*.

The cliché is that a clown longs to play Hamlet. Fine. Lemmon did become a first-rate dramatic actor, especially memorable in *Days of Wine and Roses* and *Missing*. But the clown shouldn't try to play Henry V: a funny person trying to look butch only looks ridiculous.

Walter Matthau

The Kentuckian (1955)
The Indian Fighter (1955)

"Broadway Buckeroo"

Walter Matthau has the weary voice of someone who's seen it all, a face that's appealing because it's such a shambles, and an attitude which, even on good days, can fairly be called cantankerous. No wonder he's at his best when playing put-upon New Yorkers. Shortly before his first two movies were released, Matthau was treading the boards in a role made to order for his charismatic irascibility: the slightly bewildered, marriage-shy Times Square tinhorn, Nathan Detroit, in a revival of *Guys and Dolls*.

It defies logic, but this quintessential city boy had gone off to Hollywood to play villains in a pair of Westerns. (A lone cowboy picture could have been chalked up to a single daft casting director, but *two*?) First up was *The Kentuckian*. Directed by Burt Lancaster, it's an easy-to-take tale of a frontiersman and his son who have a layover in a small hamlet to earn some money while making their way from Kentucky to Texas. Matthau, then a journeyman stage actor, didn't know much about *movie* acting when he appeared in *The Kentuckian*. He's the local saloon keeper, Stan Bodean, a pillar of the community who happens to have an unbecoming sadistic streak. Bodean takes pleasure in the little things in life, such as needling Lancaster for his lack of education and unrefined ways, and when relations between the men reach a head—it's always a dame—Matthau's weapon of choice is a bullwhip. Because we're aware of his subsequent career, the scene in which he attacks Lancaster is now hilarious. Snarling and spewing out such lines as "Next time, Wakefield, I go for the eyes," he sounds exactly like *The Odd Couple*'s Oscar Madison, if Madison had finally lost control and was trying to kill Felix Unger.

Matthau gets tied up by frontier justice in *The Indian Fighter*.
(Museum of Modern Art/Film Stills Archives)

After Matthau is done with him, Lancaster is a fright, but it is Matthau
who ultimately dies a violent death, after a couple of hooligans give him
a good whack on the noggin.

Matthau's sneering portrayal of a cravenly evil man is straight out of
a primitive tie-the-heroine-on-the-railroad-tracks silent melodrama—all
that's lacking is a mustache for him to curl. His mannerisms are so unrestrained that he mustn't have realized that on a soundstage one needn't
project all the way up to the last seat in the rear mezzanine. When he's
bellowing threats in his distinctively urban voice, it's more like the owner
of an apartment building yelling at some kids to get the hell off his stoop.
Matthau gives a large, fussy performance. He's undoubtedly trying to be

colorful, but he's merely very bad. "It was a ridiculous part," Matthau would later say. "I did it because I was desperately in need of money."

Matthau then went to work for Burt Lancaster's buddy Kirk Douglas. Starring and produced by Douglas and directed by Andre de Toth, *The Indian Fighter* is a small-scale but intense tale about a scout who tries to keep a fragile peace among the sympathetically presented Sioux, the army, and the wagon train of settlers he is leading. Matthau is a rapacious ne'er-do-well who has his heart set on plundering the Indians' "No Whites Allowed" gold mine. He does not make Douglas's life any easier and, along with his partner Lon Chaney, provokes the Indians into attacking a local army fort. But, once again, Matthau gets his in the end—a flaming arrow in the back—and with him out of the way, white man and red man acknowledge an uneasy truce.

Matthau's character isn't nearly as quirky as in *The Kentuckian* and, portraying a standard operational heavy, he's much more subdued. Still it's nearly impossible to accept him as an outdoorsman. From his facial expressions you get a sense of befuddlement, and his speaking style remains that of a New Yorker. At one point, an ad-libbing Matthau calls Chaney a "meathead," an appellation much better suited to Tenth Avenue than the Oregon Trail. Walter Matthau's penchant for gambling is well known. *The Kentuckian* and *The Indian Fighter* prove that he's much more at home betting on the horses than sitting on them. Any cheap B Western was filled with nonentities who were infinitely more convincing at cowboy stuff than this thespian imported from the Broadway stage.

MEDIEVAL MISFITS

Actors who convinced us chivalry is indeed dead

Matthew Broderick

Ladyhawke (1985)

"A Mouse Among Men"

For anyone who laments that Jerry Lewis never made a medieval comedy, there is Matthew Broderick in Richard Donner's *Ladyhawke*.

You think you've got troubles? Rutger Hauer and Michelle Pfeiffer (back in the days when she was considered just another pretty face) are lovers cursed by jealous bishop John Wood. Despite his clerical status, Wood has made a pact with the "powers of evil" in order that when the sun goes down Hauer metamorphoses from handsome knight into a wolf and at daybreak Pfeiffer turns into a hawk—hence the title. Because the two transformations take place simultaneously, he and she are never human at the same moment. Instead of making love to Pfeiffer, Hauer has to make do with having a bird perch on his arm. And so are they destined to be apart, doomed for as long as day and night are separate entities. (Good for you—you've already figured out that an eclipse is involved in setting things right.)

Broderick plays a robber who escapes from prison and hooks up with this odd couple. He does what he can to help them but, although his character (Phillipe the Mouse) is an accomplished thief, he's above all a clumsy oaf. Much of *Ladyhawke*'s footage is spent on the twenty-one-year-old Broderick falling off horses, traipsing awkwardly through the countryside, and generally acting in an infantile fashion, all the while prattling on to himself, to animals, and to God. Although he speaks in a

Matthew Broderick may be trying to ape Cary Grant from the climactic Mount Rushmore shot in *North by Northwest*, but the movie icon he most calls to mind in *Ladyhawke* is Jerry Lewis.

145

light British accent, the presence Broderick brings to the picture is anything but distinguished (let us not forget that in addition to Olivier and Gielgud, England gave the world Benny Hill).

Broderick's open-mouthed gawkiness and fidgety body language, his protruding teeth and hyperkinetic speaking style—punctuated with stammering, mewing noises, and little giggles—all recall the star of *CinderFella* and *The Nutty Professor*. A Jerry Lewis clone is not the worst thing to have in a movie (had he kept up with this style, Broderick might have preempted Jim Carrey). But the question is, what is it doing in *this* movie? We're in thirteenth-century France, and the rest of the cast performs with the measured speech of costume epics. Yet the frantic Broderick is making dumb jokes and cracking wise: the Borscht Belt has been transposed to the Middle Ages. Jerry Lewis frequently used to yammer, "Hey, lady!" We keep expecting Broderick to let loose with a "Hey, milady!"

When Broderick isn't hogging the spotlight, indulging in his manic capers, *Ladyhawke* has an almost grave quality to it. The unremitting bleakness of everyday peasant life, the harsh, unmerciful landscape, the pervasive gloom of a superstitious era are all evocatively conveyed. Above all, the impassioned performances of Hauer and Pfeiffer convince us that their plight is of momentous consequence. Yet all is for naught when Broderick comes bumbling along like a modern-day schnook.

Prior to appearing in *Ladyhawke*, Broderick made a splash on Broadway playing Neil Simon's young wise-guy alter ego in *Brighton Beach Memoirs*. Maybe winning a Tony award persuaded him he should use the same schtick for this film, because the Mouse bears more than a passing resemblance to the play's smart-ass Eugene. The original casting plans for *Ladyhawke* had Sean Connery playing the hero and Dustin Hoffman taking the role of the thief. Connery decided to reprise James Bond one last time instead, while Hoffman hemmed and hawed until producer-director Richard Donner simply looked elsewhere. Donner said that he cast the part after seeing *Brighton Beach Memoirs*, because Broderick "just destroyed me. I said, 'He's going to change the whole story, but it will make it so much richer, cleaner, fresher.' He brought a very fresh naive approach to the role." So that's what it was supposed to be.

As it turned out, several years later Sean Connery and Dustin Hoffman did act together in *Family Business*, with Matthew Broderick also part of the mix. It was a raging shambles.

Richard Gere

First Knight (1995)

"...But You Can Call Me Lance"

On paper, Richard Gere as Sir Lancelot sounds like a viable idea. One of the more resilient male sex symbols, Gere was first declared a heart-throb in the late seventies and has kept it up for two decades. But come on, Richard, put a little effort into it.

Gere seems to think he can get by with just strutting his stuff, as though *First Knight* was actually *American Gigolo 2*. One might assume that these days an actor portraying Lancelot would attempt at least an approximation of a French accent and a feeling for the period in which he's supposed to exist. But in this case one would be disappointed. When, in the opening of *First Knight*, Gere's Lancelot takes wagers for sword duels, he sounds like a local poolroom hustler. And when Guinevere comes on the scene, this Lancelot is full of sexual swagger, sounding like a lounge lizard with lame pickup lines. Nor does the script help him sound as though he lives in the sixth century. Richard Gere might say, "I can tell when a woman wants me. I can see it in her eyes," but Sir Lancelot never would.

Generally, Gere's performances over the years have had an air of slight sarcasm and arrogance that distances him from the emotional life of his characters. In *First Knight*, his trademark smirk is firmly in place, even though self-satisfaction should be anathema to a tender gallant like Lancelot. Through Gere's off-the-cuff manner, Lancelot becomes a wastrel, a bloke who, if he can't have the Queen of Camelot, will just move on to the next kingdom and find another queen. The actor himself said, "In this film, Lancelot is emotionally damaged," as though he should be enrolled in a twelve-step program.

147

Richard Gere takes time out from preening to get medieval.

Not that the failure of this movie is entirely Gere's fault. *First Knight*, with its irritatingly coy title, is a rethinking of the Arthurian legend rendered pointless because it was made by people without a lot on their minds. Merlin and Mordred are gone, but the most keenly felt absence is a sense of passion among the three main characters, whose entire relationship has been revamped. Lancelot is no longer Arthur's special favorite, his surrogate son; he's just another guy sitting at the Round Table. When Lancelot first stumbles across Guinevere, he hasn't even met the king and she isn't yet Arthur's wife. Since we're not given a Lancelot who falls in love with the woman married to the man he reveres, there is no resonance in his feelings and no tension in the interactions among the trio. As Arthur, Sean Connery has the bored demeanor of someone who's seen it all before, and in the person of Julia Ormond, Guinevere doesn't have enough screen presence to be believable as a woman who arouses the passion of one man, let alone two.

Director Jerry Zucker first gained notice with his movie spoofs (*Airplane*, for one), but he's often funnier when he's trying to be serious. (Who can forget the evil spirits coming to whisk Tony Goldwyn off to hell at the end of *Ghost*?) What could have transpired in conversations between Zucker and his production designer? The Camelot of *First Knight* is an otherwise average-looking medieval city differentiated from all other such cities by the goofy pastel blue roofs on the buildings. Zucker said the look of *First Knight* was "vaguely medieval": "We're not trying for authenticity. I took the line that as long as they don't have pop-up toasters and microwave ovens we aren't that bothered. I mean, if you want to do Ingmar Bergman what you end up with is a film where everybody is covered in shit, and who wants that?" But who would want *First Knight*—a love story devoid of romance?

Alan Ladd

The Black Knight (1954)

"Little Man, What Now?"

Alan Ladd was most at home in a trenchcoat, looking warily over his shoulder on a rainy, nighttime urban street. He also acquitted himself well with boots and saddles. His laconic manner was perfectly suited both to the inherent cynicism of film noir and the loner qualities of Western heroes. One place he should have stayed far away from, though, was Camelot. Knights are supposed to be buoyant, dashing, spirited. Taciturnity is frankly unbecoming in King Arthur's England.

British-made, *The Black Knight* was one of the least of the medieval adventure movies that enjoyed a vogue in the early fifties in the wake of *Ivanhoe*'s success. Ladd's foray into the genre was a threadbare affair, juvenalia about a scheme hatched by a nefarious Saracen Knight of the Round Table (huh?) and a Cornish king in which their followers are disguised as Vikings to rid England of both Christianity and its most prominent communicant: King Arthur. Ladd has a Jones for Patricia Medina, which is too bad for him because he's a mere village smitty—albeit the greatest swordmaker in the whole wide world—while she's the daughter of an earl, and this is England, where they've got that class distinction thing. So when her pop catches them smooching, he gives the short-of-stature Ladd the bum's rush.

Medina is a liberal of the "We're All God's Children" school, but her devotion to Ladd fades when her family estate is attacked by the villains in their Viking outfits; because she sees him running away from the castle during the attack, she jumps to the conclusion that her beau is yellow. But Alan Ladd would never be so pusillanimous—he was simply chasing some of the hooligans who were fleeing the scene of the crime.

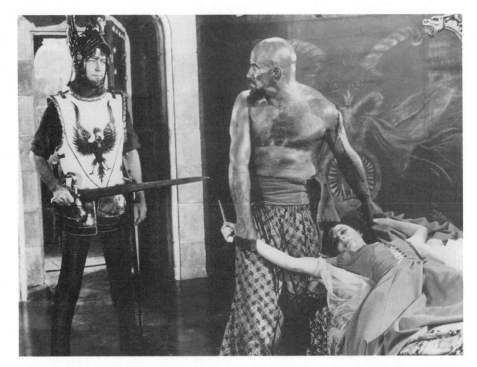

Would Alan Ladd have traveled all the way to England to make *The Black Knight* if he knew he would end up looking this silly? That's some sword he's packing, or is he just happy to see Patricia Medina?

To get the goods on the bad guys and regain Medina's affection, Ladd reappears disguised in the raiment of the film's title character. (His armor *is* black, but given the dominance of an ornithological motif on his breastplate and helmet, perhaps this movie should have been called *The Rooster Man*.)

The movie's choicest moments come when it ventures to address the question of how Stonehenge got that way. It seems the place served as the open-air temple for heliolatrous rituals, and the viewer is privileged to witness a solemn ceremony in which a gaggle of temple dancers—overage chorines who look like they were shipped in from some cheesy music hall in Brighton—kick up their heels prior to the sacrosanct rite of monk-barbecuing. The kidnapped Medina is also going to be sacrificed under the knife, but not before a crone covers the maiden's dark locks with a peroxide blond wig (not an easy thing to come by in the sixth century).

The rationale given for this coiffure choice is that the sun gods demand that their sacrifices be "flaxen-haired." The actual explanation, however, is that when *The Black Knight* was made, Marilyn Monroe was the hottest female star in the world, so it was presumed that adolescent boys would be more titillated by a woman writhing on a slab, cleavage bursting through her bodice, if she had platinum hair—it also added an alluring air of tawdriness. As Medina is about to get hers, the heroic Black Knight thunders onto the scene to save the day. He frees the monks and carries off his beloved as King Arthur's knights come storming in just like the U.S. Cavalry. Once the pagans are dispatched with, a disgusted Arthur orders, "Destroy this evil place. Scatter the stones and let them lie as witness in the years to come of heaven's wrath against the evil practiced here." And that's why to this day buses still line up at Salisbury Plain in Wiltshire, and gawking tourists take photographs of a bunch of old stones.

In plot, dialogue and characterization, *The Black Knight* operates solely on a comic-book level and has almost no relation to the Arthurian legend; there's not even a passing reference to Lancelot. The film was clumsily put together by the genial veteran Tay Garnett, who throughout his career had a tendency, when all else failed, to rely on rowdiness to get over the rough spots. *The Black Knight* is filled with lots of shots of rowdy horsemen. Who they are and where they're heading is not always clear.

Poor Ladd. Seeing an established movie star so ill at ease is painful. His movements tend to be clipped and tentative, at odds with the swashbuckling heroics he was asked to perform. The rest of the cast is British, and the juxtaposition of Ladd's flat accent and achromatic line readings against their histrionic orations is rather like coming across a single slice of Kraft American Cheese in the middle of a platter of Stilton. Moreover, Ladd seems out of place visually: all of the character actors surrounding him have striking, long angular faces, his is round and puffy. And his unbecoming long locks make him look as though he were the Pennsylvania Dutch Boy grown old. Writing in faux Olde English, the critic from *Time* called Ladd, "the most onnatural knight that ever was my doule to see."

Robert Wagner

Prince Valiant (1954)

"Wigged Out"

It's bad enough for an actor to be stuck with a role he's obviously unsuited for, but much worse when he's given the appearance of a complete buffoon. Robert Wagner was a baby-faced young man who became a favorite of the saddle-shoe set after playing a shell-shocked soldier who is cured when serenaded by Susan Hayward in *With a Song in My Heart*. A pleasant Joe College–type, he had no business impersonating the hero of Harold Foster's long-running comic strip—a Scandinavian prince having adventures in Arthurian England.

If 20th Century–Fox didn't want to be bombarded with complaints from disgruntled comic-strip readers, the first thing the studio had to do was make sure that the movie's Prince Valiant looked like their hero. This meant that the actor playing the role would have to sport the character's trademark haircut. (Prince Valiant without his page boy would be like Little Orphan Annie with pupils.) It's unfortunate that satisfying a cartoon readership resulted in making the star of the movie look like a ninny—no one in the world could have maintained a sense of dignity in the wig foisted upon Robert Wagner. During *Prince Valiant*, you wonder why Val (as his friends call him) would have chosen this hairdo: Nobody else in the movie has a mane that looks anything like his, so it's not as if the Dutch Boy was all the sixth-century rage. Why doesn't one of his friends take him aside and suggest that maybe he should consider going with a different look? How could Janet Leigh fall for someone so goofy? (And while we're at it, why, in the comic strip, if Valiant is Scandinavian, does he have coal-black hair, anyway?) Robert Wagner would later look back and laugh at the movie he called "my worst bomb." He recounted that

Dean Martin ran into him on the studio lot and that "[o]bserving the black wig and bangs, he talked to me for ten minutes before he realized I wasn't Jane Wyman."

If Prince Valiant's hair diminishes Robert Wagner's masculinity quotient, his taste in clothes doesn't exactly restore it. His sleeveless frock resembles nothing so much as a girl's pinafore from the mid-fifties. What Wagner most brings to mind is a young man at an all-male college who, as a good sport, plays the female lead in a drama club production. (The contrast between his girlish appearance and his athletic feats—climbing, swinging on ropes, jumping, brandishing a sword—is quite humorous.)

You have to give Robert Wagner some credit: He wore this wig and still managed to have a career.

Robert Wagner was twenty-three when he made *Prince Valiant* and his acting ability was, to put it gently, inchoate. If you read the *Prince Valiant* comic strip, you imagine an eloquent hero speaking in sonorous tones. In the movie, you get a callow, atonic Wagner yapping, "The cross is our salvation. You'll burn in hell!" and sounding like a peevish schoolboy. Your heart goes out because he's trying to hold his own against James Mason, and it's no contest. Since Val is in the midst of the knights of King Arthur's Round Table, Wagner is often addressing others as "Sir." When he does, the image of a college campus is once again conjured up, with Wagner a student who's full of golly-gee! enthusiasm and asking all sorts of questions of his professor.

HOW WE WON THE WAR

*Some unlikely spies in the battle against Hitler
and the Axis powers*

This is how Joan Crawford registers disdain. A former society girl, she's reduced to selling haute couture to the obnoxious wives of Nazi officers in occupied Paris. In this case, it's Natalie Schaefer, who would later gain immortality as *Gilligan's Island*'s Mrs. Thurston Howell III. (Museum of Modern Art/Film Stills Archives)

Joan Crawford

Reunion in France (1943)

"An American in Paris"

In *Reunion in France*, Joan Crawford portrays a woman who is a) rich, b) Parisienne, and c) involved with the French Resistance. Is she believable in any of these modes? The answers are a) moderately, b) nope, and c) are you kidding?

Although she was playing an heiress, Crawford's attempt to act upper class ends up not so much Old Money as Publisher's Clearing House sweepstakes winner. Of course, nouveau riche is what Crawford was. Having come from hardscrabble roots, the actress doesn't have the easy, self-assured carriage of someone who grew up in wealth. This deficiency is not critical because you *are* able to detect, in nascent form, Crawford's caustic cruelty and hard-edged imperiousness, traits that fully blossomed soon after and which her daughter Christina chronicled so colorfully in *Mommie Dearest*. Through these qualities, the actress conveys a haughty disdain for others that is appropriate for her character in the early parts of *Reunion in France*. She sometimes strains too much to sound patrician—"neither" is inevitably pronounced "neye-ther"—but it's irresistible to witness Joan Crawford having a go at lines like "You hear so little Mendelssohn these days" and "Isn't that the march from *Die Meistersinger*? . . . But that's Hitler's favorite march!"

As for sounding French, though, she hardly seems to be trying. Her accent is, at best, fitful: every ten minutes or so, you can detect a *soupçon* of *français* in her voice. Because Crawford's Parisian impersonation is a washout (especially in contrast to that of her Dutch-born costar, Philip Dorn, who, though he may have been a low-rent Charles Boyer, got Frenchspeak down pat), her character would seem to be more at home strolling down Michigan Avenue than the Champs-Elysées. And then there's the espionage business: Who else but Joan Crawford would be fleeing the Nazis while wearing an ultrachic fur coat complete with shoulder pads?

In *Reunion in France*, Crawford is Michèle de la Becque. Chic, pampered, and bored, she pays no attention to World War II, which has yet to hit France, but just you wait. Michèle goes on a trip to the shore, and her holiday is ruined when Hitler invades France. Dodging attacks by German planes and witnessing the slaughter of people around her, Michèle walks back to her hometown just like a refugee except that she is wearing costumes by Irene and Joan Crawford "fuck-me" shoes. In Paris she gets her dander up when she finds that the family mansion has been taken over by the Nazis for a coal allotment center, thus subjecting her to the indignation of having to sleep in the concierge's room.

Now dedicated to Mother France and Liberty, Equality, and Fraternity, Michèle is disgusted to learn that her industrial designer boyfriend, Robert (Dorn), has become a Nazi collaborator and that his plants are building planes and tanks for the German army. This gives Joan ample opportunity to simmer and steam, to glare and arch her eyebrows. Her money gone, the former *mondaine* is forced to take a job at the haute couturier where she used to spend a fortune, working as a fitter's assistant with the shopgirls to whom she had once acted so imperiously. Her mettle is further tested when she hides brash Pat Talbot (John Wayne), a wounded R.A.F.(!) pilot from Wilkes-Barre who has escaped from a concentration camp. So strong is her devotion to the cause that she even necks with a loathsome Nazi officer so that Pat and a Resistance fighter will escape detection. Michèle orchestrates Pat's escape to England through a ruse in which the American pretends to be her chauffeur, but she decides not to join him. She has learned that far from being a despicable quisling, Robert is the head of the greatest Resistance organization in all of France. (Those tanks and trucks his factories make for the Nazis—he designed them to be gas guzzling lemons.) Michèle knows that her place is in Paris. With Robert. At the fade-out, she modestly tells him, "I won't be much help, I know. But you won't be quite as lonely."

Never an especially political person—she did donate an ambulance to the Loyalists in the Spanish Civil War, but that was mostly due to the influence of her husband at the time, the left-leaning Franchot Tone—Crawford's patriotic awakening in *Reunion in France* is none too convincing. (She was much more persuasive on-screen when she could relate to the ideals her character was fighting for. Take, for example, *The Women*'s Crystal Allen, who uses her "feminine wiles" to escape her hard-knock existence: now *that* was a role Crawford could understand.) Joan's reactions to Nazi terrorism come closer to petulance and irritation than moral outrage. Her heroics are a teensy bit ridiculous, but she does them all totally straight-faced. (Even after her character is penniless, Joan wears a different stylish outfit in almost every scene.)

Joan Crawford and John Wayne are such distinctive and usually dominant individuals that having them together on-screen is jarring, as though one of them walked onto the wrong soundstage. And although neither had formal training, their styles are discordant: Crawford is very clearly *acting*, while Wayne is relying upon his personality. It's just as well that contrary to expected film conventions, they don't end up together at the end of the movie.

Reunion in France is dopey, but it's not unamusing. Before being blacklisted and going to Europe in the late forties and turning pretentious, director Jules Dassin could be counted on to keep things moving, and this film is never boring. As presented here, Occupied Paris is not such a bad place, and the worst trait of the Germans is their boorishness. It's borderline offensive, I suppose, that the height of Nazi evil is shown to be the rude, mostly fat German women who push and shove looking for bargains at the dress salon where Crawford is working. But it is also pretty funny: a petite French woman is demoted to salesperson after the Germans come to town because "mannequins are running to larger sizes now."

Years later, Crawford had this to say about *Reunion in France*: "Oh, God. If there is an afterlife, and I am to be punished for my sins, this is one of the pictures they'll make me see over and over again. John Wayne and I both went down for the count, not just because of a silly script, but because we were so mismatched. Get John out of the saddle and you've got trouble."

Melanie Griffith

Shining Through (1992)

"A Dim Light"

Thanks to a new Nazi secret weapon, every Allied soldier is in peril. Whom are you going to send to Europe to save the day? Melanie Griffith, of course.

In *Shining Through*, Griffith plays a young woman from Queens who, although half Jewish, has been told by her family to pass herself off as Irish. Because her diploma reads "the Queens Clerical College" rather than "Vassar," she's at first turned down for a terrific secretarial position at an old-line New York law firm. (If anything should have kept her from being hired, it's her annoying little girl's voice. Who'd want to have to listen to that for eight hours a day?) But when the lawyers find out she's proficient in German—an invaluable skill in a firm with an international practice in 1940—she gets the job. (Melanie's beloved Papa spoke German at home, hence the skill, and hence, unfortunately, the rest of the movie.)

She works for a partner referred to as "the pallbearer" because he never smiles, although, as Michael Douglas plays him, he's a pretty blithe fellow from the get-go. True to movie conventions, however, he is not what he seems, and inveterate film buff Melanie has seen enough suspense pictures to comprehend straightaway that her boss is an American spy. Michael is impressed by her savvy, and soon thereafter Melanie confides to the audience that "by day we worked together, at night we were lovers." Their idyll is destroyed when, osculating in bed on December 7, 1941, they hear that America is at war.

Things are looking grim for our side. The Germans are developing "a bomb that can fly by itself," and the crackerjack spy who had been getting the lowdown on the weapon has been found out and hanged. His

Melanie Griffith displays what the well-dressed undercover spy is wearing in Nazi Germany this season. A smitten Liam Neeson watches her instead of the opera.

espionage technique was to pose as a fabulous dress designer and use his chic creations to ingratiate himself to the wife of an up-and-coming Nazi officer; while at her place for fittings, he'd photograph the secret papers hubby left lying around. (*Shining Through* constantly scrimps on plausibility.) So what the Allies need is someone else who can make house calls. Malapert Melanie pipes up that she's the one who should go, on account of the fact that she speaks German and can pose as a cook. Never mind that she has had no training in cloak-and-dagger work. Douglas makes only the most perfunctory protestations, and she's off to Berlin.

Our Melanie's culinary skills turn out to be woeful, and she promptly louses up a dinner party given by the targeted Nazi. But it just so happens that Liam Neeson—playing a Bad (albeit civilized) German a year before he became Good German Oskar Schindler—takes a shine to her and hires her as a nanny. Better still, he's a Nazi party bigwig, and on that very night has been given the secret papers that Melanie is trying to sniff out. She's the kind of spy who photographs the documents in the basement with all the lights on while Neeson is upstairs, so it's not surprising that she's soon fleeing, running from Potsdam to Berlin in an evening gown and high heels.

Duty makes her kill a German agent, and soon the Gestapo is dogging her trail. Luckily, Michael Douglas is around to help her out: this supposedly brilliant intelligence agent comes into Germany posing as an S.S. officer *even though he doesn't speak a word of German*. They both get shot, but not to worry, they live to get married and raise a couple of sons, and she even gets to recite the whole preposterous story for a BBC documentary.

What kind of woman would be so dedicated to American ideals and so abhorred by what the Nazis are doing to the Jews that she'd be willing to put a comfortable, secure existence on the line? Logic tells us she would possess a singularity of purpose and an almost obsessive dedication to a cause, indicating that her salient quality would be solemnity. Melanie Griffith's demeanor is that of a frisky sexpot, and even when she makes a somber statement like "I'm a Jew.... I have relatives still hiding," her breathy elocution makes her sound like a pigeon cooing. There's not a great deal of gravity to this woman.

What should the O.S.S. be looking for in an agent being sent on a top-secret spy mission (apart from the preparation and experience that Griffith's character is lacking)? If the secret plan was to seduce a German general, then maybe Griffith's coquettish sensuality would come in handy. More likely, the overriding attributes would be intelligence and resolve. Melanie Griffith may be a very bright woman, but on-screen she comes off as a great big baby doll. Sigourney Weaver, Mary Stuart Masterson, and Debra Winger (who was originally slated for the role) are among those who possess the appropriate characteristics for the role, although no one could have offset the inanities with which writer-director David Seltzer infused *Shining Through*.

The film that best showcased Griffith, *Working Girl*, succeeded because her character used her kittenish qualities to undermine the expectations of others. In *Shining Through*, the actress has the same coy traits that she had in *Working Girl*, but everyone else is oblivious to them. And that's one of the reasons this movie is a piece of junk.

Fred MacMurray

Above Suspicion (1943)

"Addled Academic"

The same year that Fred MacMurray made *Above Suspicion*, he also starred in the romantic comedy *No Time for Love*, playing a sandhog—a tunnel excavator—whose rough-hewn ways win over prim news photographer Claudette Colbert. This was perfect casting for MacMurray: a no-nonsense take-charge kind of fellow, someone who acts on instinct, not intellect. *Above Suspicion* is a whole other story.

Retroactively, the primary image most of us have of the actor is as the phlegmatic head of the Douglas household in TV's *My Three Sons*, but way back when, he was a most affable leading man. In romantic triangles, Fred MacMurray was inevitably the two-fisted, upright guy who stole the girl from the effete prig with whom she had been silly enough to be smitten. He was adept at acting virile and at acting befuddled—and in his best performance, *Double Indemnity*, did both. What MacMurray didn't have on-screen was brains. And in *Above Suspicion* he is an Oxford don. The likable actor perhaps might have been able to get by as a genial professor at a little junior college, but here he's teaching at one of the world's great universities. Parents of his students should have demanded a refund of their tuition money. The movie did stop short of trying to palm him off as British—he's an American who had been a Rhodes scholar, an achievement which doesn't add to the credibility quotient.

At least MacMurray has no classroom scenes in *Above Suspicion*. When the film starts, he has just gotten married on campus to Joan Crawford. His students mischievously chain the couple's car to a post as the two are leaving on their honeymoon, but apart from running into a couple of old chums from his school days, that's it for academia. The remainder

Oxford don Fred MacMurray finds that saving his wife, Joan
Crawford, is all in a day's work when you play at spying
against the Nazis.

of the film is a byzantine suspense story in which, as a lark, the newly-
weds engage in a spot of espionage work for the British secret service.
Traveling through France and Germany, Fred and Joan do their darnedest
to locate a mysterious agent who has the lowdown on a new German
secret weapon—a magnetic mine. An ad for the film advised, "Get Your
Goose Pimples Ready! Because the suspense is terrific when moonlight
romance runs across moonlight murder!" For a more accurate idea of the
film, picture Nick and Nora Charles of *The Thin Man* without the wit or
sophistication.

Above Suspicion is fairly incomprehensible, with Joan's hat serving
as a secret password, hidden codes conveyed through a Liszt concerto, and

the couple disguised in old-age getups. As hard to swallow as all this is, the greatest implausibility remains Fred MacMurray's pedagogy. (Because Crawford's character is not well delineated—essentially no more than just a young wife—she's perfectly fine for the demands of the role.) Mac-Murray goes into a bookstore and says that he's looking for an "1836 edition of Schiller's plays," and he doesn't seem to have any idea what he's talking about. Throughout, he has a quizzical look etched upon his face—he may have intended this to be the inquisitive mien of a spy—but he merely comes across as screwy, most especially when he has donned leder-hosen. (The *New York Herald Tribune* declared that MacMurray didn't "look quite bright enough to unravel the tangled skeins of this screen melodrama.") While the Nazis under Conrad Veidt are portrayed as vicious and cruel—there are even references to Dachau—they are also seen as boobs. In one emblematic scene, MacMurray addresses one haughty Gestapo member as "dope"; the flustered swine turns to another German and asks, "*Vas heisst das 'dope'?*"

MGM had, for some reason, borrowed MacMurray from Paramount for *Above Suspicion*—as though it couldn't have found anyone equally improbable for the role among its own contract list. After this sojourn he returned home to his usual studio and better things. For Joan Crawford, however, *Above Suspicion* marked the end of an era. Disheartened by the quality of scripts she had been given of late, she asked out of her contract after eighteen years at MGM. Crawford said that if people thought that *Above Suspicion* and her previous *Reunion in France* were bad, "you should have seen the ones I went on suspension *not* to make!"

DON'T GIVE UP THE DAY JOB

Three men—of varying talents—from the world of pop music who were at sea when playing against type in rare film appearances

Tony Bennett

The Oscar (1966)

"I Left My Talent in the Recording Studio"

"**Y**ou lie down with pigs, you come up smelling like garbage." Once you've seen *The Oscar*, these words will remain lodged in your memory as an immediately identifiable and incontrovertible part of Tony Bennett, as intrinsic as "I Left My Heart in San Francisco."

Movies as unremittingly bad as *The Oscar* are rare and they must be cherished. The film charts the rise and fall of movie star Frankie Fane, who is that stock figure of trash fiction: a "heel" (a nicely evocative word that unfortunately has dropped out of the vernacular). Frankie is a force of nature and he will not be denied. We have to take it on faith that on-screen Frankie has that certain *je ne sais quoi* known as star quality because we never actually see him acting. But if Frankie is anything like Stephen Boyd, who plays him, then he's a mush-mouthed hamola. Frankie is brutish, arrogant, self-absorbed, abusive with women and contumelious to men, so his bad karma eventually catches up with him: The film star is reduced to auditioning for a television series. But then a deus ex machina in the form of an unexpected Oscar nomination for an arty box-office flop allows him to escape that fate.

The Oscar race provides Frankie with the opportunity to give his ruthlessness full rein. Placing ads in the trade papers and chatting with Johnny and Merv is not for him. No, Frankie's unorthodox campaign strategy is to hire private dick Ernest Borgnine in a convoluted scheme to make his

In his big scene, Tony Bennett gets tough with his no-good best friend Stephen Boyd, as Elke Sommer looks on in amazement. The two men give epically inept performances—Boyd by chewing the scenery as if there's no tomorrow, Bennett by not acting at all.

fellow Best Actor contenders—including "Richard Burton for *Grapes of Winter*" and "Burt Lancaster for *The Spanish Armada*"—look bad; when his plot begins to backfire, Frankie figures a murder might be just the ticket to give him front-runner status. Because producer Clarence Greene and director Russell Rouse were Oscar winners themselves—for the original story of *Pillow Talk*, no less—there was no way their movie was going to imply that an Academy Award could be won on anything other than merit. And so the Best Actor Oscar, presented by Merle Oberon, goes not to Frankie Fane but to Frank Sinatra.

The Oscar features an all–semi-star cast and the requisite array of stereotyped women with whom Frankie sleeps on his way to the top (including Elke Sommer, Jill St. John, and Eleanor Parker). It is, however, Tony Bennett's amateur-night theatrics that put *The Oscar* into the pantheon of camp classics. He's Frankie's best friend and lackey, the piquantly named Hymie Kelly (his parents, he explains, were Mike Kelly and Sadie Rabinowitz). For most of the picture, Hymie is a Frankie Fane wannabe, a slow traveler in the fast lane. Unlike Frankie, he's not completely bereft of morals, but he still basks in the reflected sleaze of the master and he's equally dedicated to hedonism, always on the lookout for "a swinging party in the Village, with lots of chicks . . . Man, what a scene!" (Hymie is forever spouting fifties hipster slang—in the sixties.)

As a singer, Tony Bennett expresses, more than anything, an even-keeled humanism, his unaffected style manifesting sagaciousness and empathy. (If Frank Sinatra is the grandiose romantic, Bennett's warm manner is that of a clear-eyed pragmatist who has a reserve of optimism.) His calling card as a musical performer is simple down-to-earth decency. Untrained as an actor, Bennett doesn't even begin to create a characterization in *The Oscar*. Essentially, he's himself on the screen, so it's impossible to accept him as the crony of a creep like Frankie Fane. You're convinced that the real Tony would have simply gotten up and left the room when Frankie walked in. It's astonishing, though, just how inept Bennett is here.

Singing, Bennett's urbane and eloquent. Trying to act, he becomes a palooka. In *The Oscar*, he's just a guy reciting words by rote, his delivery unmodulated, his cadences haphazard, with accents and emphases adopted willy-nilly, as though he's winging it as he goes along. There's no game plan to Bennett's performance: he rushes through some long speeches in a single breath and at other times lingers agonizingly over short lines. Bennett often speaks sotto voce, giving the impression that subconsciously he didn't want people to hear what he was saying. In his big scene, a drunk and tearful Hymie finally stands up to Frankie: "I'm nothing but a parasite . . . I've let you castrate me inch by inch. I'm weak. I'm a leech." It's a toss-up as to which is less convincing, the drunkenness or the self-debasement.

Bennett was also given a unique expletive in *The Oscar*; since "Bullshit" was taboo in the cinema of 1966, he was forced to exclaim "Birdseed!" He's at his most unforgettable, though, with the "You lie down with pigs, you come up smelling like garbage" aphorism, spoken after he learns of Frankie's Oscar campaign machinations. The ludicrousness of this crude maxim is matched by the half-baked intensity in Bennett's voice. He gets to reprise the line a few minutes later when Frankie is panicking about getting nailed for his intrigue; this time, his reading is more reflective, but he still speaks with an utter lack of conviction. During filming, Bennett claimed to be amazed at how true to life *The Oscar* was: "Every place I go, I hear dialogue from the script." (Which lines? Stephen Boyd's "You've got a glass head. I can see right through it. That's how I know you're stupid"? Or Eleanor Parker's "I don't know why I keep expecting you to act like other men when you're not. You're another kind of machine entirely"?)

Tony Bennett's participation in *The Oscar* was a casting gimmick not uncommon in the fifties and sixties: to get people talking, showy roles in dramas were given to performers associated with comedy or music. (Frank Sinatra's role in *From Here to Eternity* is the most celebrated example.) Naturally, production notes for the film gushed that Bennett's screen test resulted in "a role in *The Oscar* which can easily make him a candidate for one." Not quite. The critic for *Cue* quipped that Bennett "would have been better advised to spend the time rummaging around San Francisco looking for his heart." *The Oscar* remains, mercifully, Bennett's one stab at acting. If he had kept it up, it's doubtful he would have experienced his remarkable cross-generational reincarnation in the 1990s as the coolest man on earth.

Liberace

Sincerely Yours (1955)

"Deaf and Very Dumb"

Florid and unnervingly unctuous, Liberace was a decidedly strange phenomenon of the mid-fifties. Somebody at Warner Bros. reckoned that since his audience (mainly older women) couldn't seem to get enough of the flamboyant, wavy-haired pianist on television, where he engaged in genial conversation, gave off his toothy smile, and played—critics would say assaulted—his instrument, surely they'd be eager to see two hours of him on the big screen in full color. But did the studio really think that the American public was so naive that it would accept Liberace as a man involved with *two* women? Granted, one of his leading ladies in *Sincerely Yours* was Dorothy Malone, who had made her mark playing a nympho-maniac in *The Big Sleep* (and would win an Oscar for playing another one in *Written on the Wind*), but still . . .

Maybe Liberace's fans felt that the intimate one-on-one relationship they had with him on television would be lost if they sat in a theater filled with others of their ilk. Perhaps they were like a group of matrons in the movie who are crestfallen when they see him kiss a young woman: His public didn't want to consider Liberace and sex as having anything to do with each other. (One of the most appealing aspects of Liberace was that he was a gentleman, i.e., he didn't seem to think about such things.) Or maybe they could sense just how awful a movie *Sincerely Yours* is. For whatever reason, the film was a box-office disaster.

Movies don't come much more shameless than *Sincerely Yours*, a remake of an old George Arliss vehicle, *The Man Who Played God*. Lib-erace plays a pianist who is about to make the leap from popular favorite ("You give pleasure and comfort to the millions," his manager, William

That Liberace, unaccustomed as he was, had to decide between *two* women—Dorothy Malone or Joanne Dru—is merely one of the preposterous elements of *Sincerely Yours*.

Demarest, assures him) to serious artist via a Carnegie Hall debut. Of all the dumb luck, just as he is about to take the stage, he goes deaf.

To fill up his lonely hours, the pianist takes up lipreading. That's when *Sincerely Yours* really gets going. On his apartment terrace high above Fifth Avenue, Liberace spies on people in Central Park through binoculars, "eavesdropping" on their conversations. Daily, he keeps his eyes glued on a crippled boy who can only watch while the other fellas play football. Seeing the pathetic lad is upsetting to the sensitive Liberace, and he admits that the one-two punch of his own situation and that of the boy's "makes me wonder, wonder about God. A God who hasn't time, hasn't time to help anyone who needs him." Liberace follows the youngster to church and hears him talk to God. "I know you got lots on your mind, and maybe I shouldn't be reminding you," the boy prays, as a heavenly chorus fills the soundtrack. "But you know, I missed football season last year and I kind of thought you'd help me this year. But so far, well, I missed the first two games. I guess you've just been too busy." The next time Liberace eavesdrops, the crippled boy is telling his grandfather that he's giving up on this prayer business. This will never do, and Liberace arranges to pay for an operation. Before you know it, the boy is a quarterback.

The pianist's other charity case is straight from *Queen for a Day*. A humble woman's daughter married rich but is ashamed to have Mom over to the mansion in Westchester. So daughter meets mother in the park and gives her cash. Liberace dubs the situation "a small American tragedy." He makes things right, though, by buying the woman a new wardrobe and giving her a complete makeover, in a sequence that was specifically designed to melt the hearts of his core audience.

Lee's voyeurism inadvertently reveals the truth about his fianceé, Dorothy Malone, for, on Christmas Eve, he lip-reads her words of love to her new beau, as well as her insistence that she's obligated to stay with her deaf fiancé. Being the nice guy he is, Liberace graciously sets her free to follow her heart. Emboldened by the St. Christopher medal the formerly crippled boy gives him, Liberace decides to undergo the high-risk operation that just might restore his hearing. There are some tense moments, but, of course, the procedure is a success. His secretary, Joanne Dru, is waiting for him with loving arms, and he finally makes his triumphant Carnegie Hall debut.

Perhaps the most damning thing you can say about Liberace's performance is that it's in keeping with the quality of his material. He is playing both himself and the character, and he doesn't do right by either. Whatever it was that Liberace had, on television he presented it with self-assurance. In *Sincerely Yours*, he's largely being Liberace: his whiny voice and oleaginous manner are front and center, but because he's using them to say the scripted lines of a fictional character, the inexperienced actor is wooden and monotonous. (Liberace had appeared in two previous movies. He performed his act in 1951's *Footlight Varieties*, a hodgepodge of musical numbers and old film clips hosted by Jack Paar. In the 1950 drama, *South Sea Sinner*, his pianist character was more or less Dooley Wilson to Shelley Winters's Humphrey Bogart.) At one point in *Sincerely Yours* he does get to let loose: The scene in which he realizes he's losing his hearing is done without sound, giving Lee the opportunity to perform with all the exaggerated emoting of a very bad silent-movie actor.

The hero in *Sincerely Yours* is the idol of millions. The ladies think he's dreamy. Men are filled with respect for his artistry. Girls want to marry him when they grow up, boys want to be him. This is all highly unlikely given the mincing manner in which Liberace portrays the character. It's an unspeakably noble part, and for there to have been any credibility at all, the character needed to evince a certain degree of suaveness and savoir faire. Liberace does no such thing.

The main problem with Liberace at this point in his career was that he was so damned sincere. Later, though, he developed a mischievously self-deprecating sense of humor and became almost lovable; he was very funny when he appeared in his final movie ten years later, playing a coffin salesman in Tony Richardson's *The Loved One*. And as proof that he no longer took himself too seriously, his appearance as a presenter at the 1981 Academy Awards was prefaced by a clip of the opening credits to *Sincerely Yours*. "I've done my part for motion pictures," joked Liberace. "I've stopped making them."

Johnnie Ray

There's No Business Like Show Business (1954)

"God Works in Mysterious Ways"

Johnnie Ray, who was all the rage in the early fifties, is sometimes called the missing link between Frank Sinatra and Elvis Presley. Before Ray, crooners were happy just to stand there at the microphone and sing. Not Johnnie. He had to flail his arms wildly, bend over in feigned emotional distress, change pitch and tempo with abandon, and punctuate such songs as "Cry" and "The Little White Cloud That Cried" with anguished ululations and disconcerting facial contortions. Through these activities, he stirred the loins of teenage girls of the day, sending them into such paroxysms of delirium that parents sometimes worried. Publicists gave him sobriquets like "The Prince of Wails" and "The Nabob of Sob."

The older folks dismissed Ray. Although conceding that "In a field overrun by imitations and imitators, Johnnie Ray is unique," *Newsweek* decreed that his extravagant emoting "seem[s] suitable only to a man just condemned to the tortures of the damned." And Broadway columnist Earl Wilson laughed that Ray "is the wildest, craziest, looniest, goofiest, weirdest singer since Frankie Swoonatra. He gives the impression that he's having a baby, though I know positively that he isn't."

In 1954, Ray had his shot at motion picture fame. Built around some old Irving Berlin songs, *There's No Business Like Show Business* deals with a family of vaudevillians from the end of the First World War to the beginning of the Second. Each of the five members of this clan is an acquired taste: loudmouth Ethel Merman and lumpish Dan Dailey are the parents, elfin Donald O'Connor the skirt-chasing son, and chronically chipper Mitzi Gaynor the daughter. Johnnie Ray is the eldest child who, for reasons not readily apparent, decides to leave show business and become a priest.

Johnnie Ray may be stunned that someone else in *There's No Business Like Show Business* is even more histrionic than he. But as Donald O'Connor knows, when Ethel Merman lets loose, you don't try to compete. (Museum of Modern Art/Film Stills Archives)

Not that Ray had added much to the family troupe, since the core of their act was dancing. As Dan Dailey admits, the boy "was no hoofer" (though Dailey does gush that "he sure could sell a song"). Before he gets the calling for the priesthood, however, we are given a glimmer of his particular talents. Ray—all teeth and mouth—wears white tie and tails and sits at a piano, looking like the poor man's Liberace. Playing ersatz Beethoven chords, he lumbers through the beginning of "Alexander's Ragtime Band," painfully protracting each syllable, as was his wont. Then he gets up and does his Johnnie Ray thing, arms lashing out in all directions, head bobbing wildly like one of those little toy dogs people used to put by the back windshields of their cars. The man is a fracas all by himself. When the five family members join together in a processional chorus line for the number's finale, you can see what Dan Dailey meant about his son's lack of terpsichorean ability—Ray is so hepped up that none of his movements match those of the four others.

Johnnie Ray is about the least likely clergyman imaginable. Having had twelve years of Catholic education, I've seen a lot of priests in my day. They've run the gamut from the heavy-duty devout to the dandified, but not a single one was anything like Father Johnnie. Ray's performing style is so carnal and so completely self-involved that it's hard to believe he's had a single spiritual thought in his life. As an actor, Ray is flaccid in bearing, adenoidal of voice. This is not a fellow you can picture contemplating the impenetrable mystery of the Holy Trinity or questioning why an all-loving God would allow evil to flourish.

At a farewell party before he enters the seminary, the character gets to be Johnnie Ray one more time. He performs "If You Believe," a cloying treatise on how to get to heaven taken out of Irving Berlin's piano bench. Ray does this one in two modes: sitting at the piano, singing reverentially, as though lyrics such as "I'm not making promises to the doubting Thomases" were part of a profound hymn, and standing up, giving it all he's got in the manner of a rollicking gospel song. Once again, there's the tremolo in the voice, the abrupt switches in pitch, the seeming loss of motor control, and the high-strung hysterics. None of the guests at his party get anywhere near him—those thrashing arms of his are dangerous. Bosley Crowther of the *New York Times* warned that during this number "your flesh is likely to crawl."

After this, Ray is pretty much out of the picture, although he does return for the film's conclusion, back onstage with the rest of the family— and again out of step—for an encore reprise of "Alexander's Ragtime Band." At this point, Ray has become an army chaplain, which is even more implausible than his being a parish priest. Is Johnnie Ray really the person to whom the boys in the foxholes would want to bear their souls? (Only one thing about Ray's casting in this movie makes any sense: the mating of Ethel Merman and Dan Dailey might well have spawned something like him.)

Apart from Johnnie Ray's singular contributions, *There's No Business Like Show Business* is a giddy olio of prodigal production numbers, backstage hokum, corny family melodramatics, and unconvincing love stories. Donald O'Connor ends up with Marilyn Monroe—as unlikely a matchup as Johnnie Ray and the Church. Here is high drama in *There's No Business Like Show Business*: the irresponsible O'Connor ends up in the hospital after a drunk-driving accident, thus missing the opening night of the Broadway show in which he and sis Mitzi Gaynor are featured. Dan Dailey shows up at the hospital and calls his son a "punk." This so hurts O'Connor's feelings that he vanishes for a whole year, trying to learn who and what he is. This search for fulfillment leads him to the navy. Meanwhile, who should go on in O'Connor's place in the new musical? No, not his understudy. It's Ethel Merman. There are some very pointed differences between these two performers: They are of different sexes, and while Merman may have vocalized like no one else, she danced no better than you or I.

Foolish as all this is, *There's No Business Like Show Business* is nevertheless an irreplaceable document. For anyone interested in the history of American popular culture, having Johnnie Ray preserved on film is invaluable—otherwise, future generations might not have believed such a creature ever existed.

KNOTTED FAMILY TIES

Family trees that produced some very strange fruit

Is there even one physical aspect that these two women have in common, any shared feature that might lead someone to think they are mother and daughter?

Judith Anderson and Rita Hayworth

Salome (1953)

"Recessive Gene"

*S*alome was part of the seemingly endless procession of biblical epics of the early fifties, movies that aimed to give audiences the same alluring gallimaufry of sex, sadism, and saintliness that Cecil B. DeMille's *Samson and Delilah* had presented so profitably in 1949. Typical of its ilk, *Salome* is full of high-grade hamminess, but it stands out because of the genealogy found within. In the title role is Rita Hayworth: Beautiful. Glamorous. Vivacious. Her mother is played by Judith Anderson, a woman who clearly did not get by on her looks alone. Along with a theatrical grandiosity, Anderson possessed a stern mien and features that could generously be described as aquiline. A quick glance at the profiles of the two women tells you that Rita and some homely baby must have been switched at birth. At the very least, the man who fathered Hayworth would have had to be an Adonis to have been able to offset Anderson's gene pool so dramatically. The corpulent, unaesthetic Charles Laughton was cast as Hayworth's *step*father, King Herod, and not her actual sire— suspension of disbelief can only be taken so far.

Other than this odd family tree, there's not much to ponder in *Salome*. Every biblical film has its allotment of risible dialogue, and this one doesn't disappoint. Two soldiers are discussing a rumor they heard about one of Jesus's miracles: "They say he turned water into wine at a wedding in Cana. Imagine the money he would save us! Ha-ha!" The movie also contains considerable revisionism about the young lady who danced in exchange for the head of John the Baptist. As opposed to the incorrigible vixen we've come to know through more traditional interpretations, Rita Hayworth's Salome acts like a bad girl only because she doesn't know any better. All it takes is a good man like Roman commander Stewart Granger—a closet Christian—to show her the path to righteousness. So while Hayworth's Salome does indeed go into her Dance of the Seven Veils, her purpose is to ask Laughton to *spare* the Baptist. But naughty Judith Anderson gets to the king before Hayworth, and it's off with John's head, which is thrust in front of the camera when it's brought in on a platter—a rather unappetizing cinematic moment. This sight stops Hayworth dead in her tracks, which it would have had to, since the censors wouldn't have allowed her to remove her seventh veil and become buck naked.

The last time we see Hayworth, she's out on a date with Stewart Granger listening to Jesus preaching the Sermon on the Mount. In contrast to this serene scene, her mother's final moments in the film are spent cackling hysterically with crazed delight over the demise of the Baptist. Suddenly Judith Anderson has gone from playing Queen Herodias to becoming nutty Mrs. Danvers from *Rebecca* all over again.

Yul Brynner and Tony Curtis

Taras Bulba (1962)

"Contrasting Cossacks"

Think of Yul Brynner and you see a bald head. Think of Tony Curtis and you picture a man who never had a bad hair day. Hear Brynner's voice and your ears will be filled with the resonant sounds of his Russian homeland. Although by the time of *Taras Bulba* he had decreased his Bronx accent by half, Tony Curtis still gave evidence of his New York roots when he talked. If you were asked to select a popular actor in 1962 who could play Yul Brynner's son, chances are that Tony Curtis's name would come up only a little before Troy Donahue, Jerry Lewis, and Sidney Poitier.

Taras Bulba is a not-very-faithful adaptation of the Gogol novel about a sixteenth-century uprising of the Cossacks against despotic Poles. The novel is primarily a family drama set against a tumultuous historic background. The movie emphasizes the epic, with only the most facile father-and-son conflict slipped in toward the end. As would be expected, Brynner is more in his element than is his on-screen son, which only means that his screen persona more closely approximates Hollywood's version of the Cossacks. Like so many movie ethnic groups, *Taras Bulba*'s Cossacks are an inordinately boisterous bunch: dancing, boozing, brawling, laughing, expressing deep familial love, and masterfully handling a sword on horseback are their predominant traits. Brynner also possessed the physical authority and sense of passion to make him a believable rebel leader, one who can scowl and make such pronouncements as "I will kiss the devil before my son wears a Polish collar!" and "There's only one way to keep faith with a Pole: Put your faith in your sword and the sword in the Pole!"

Curtis's character, although a fierce warrior in the field, is as concerned with the daughter of the Polish governor as he is with the freedom of the Cossacks. Parts of *Taras Bulba* recall Curtis's early forays into swashbuckling, but he is immeasurably better at blending into period settings than in the days of *The Black Shield of Falworth*. He does, however, seem to be taking *Taras Bulba* less seriously than do his fellow actors.

After an hour and a half of tongue-in-cheek adventure, cavalry attacks, and celebratory parties, Curtis turns his back on his own people in order to save his Polish girlfriend. An enraged and anguished Brynner forces a showdown, but what was heartrending in Gogol becomes inconsequential. It's hard to get worked up over a conflict between father and son when the principals couldn't even pass as second cousins.

Father and son go into their dance.

Sean Connery, Dustin Hoffman, and Matthew Broderick

Family Business (1989)

"Harebrained Heredity"

If you were making a movie that delved into the relationships among three generations of a family and touched upon the issue of how heredity affects personality, wouldn't you try to cast it with actors who looked like they might be related? The people behind *Family Business* came up with this grouping: father Sean Connery, son Dustin Hoffman, and grandson Matthew Broderick. Perhaps they thought that starpower would render the absurdity of this proposed bloodline irrelevant.

Once this trio was signed, the preposterousness of the situation must have become apparent, because the dialogue is frequently placing blame on the women Connery and Hoffman married for causing the gene pool to get jumbled. The complete ethnic makeup is as follows: Connery is 100 percent Scottish. He married a Sicilian and produced Hoffman, who is therefore half-Scottish and half-Italian, but looks neither. Hoffman's wife is Jewish, making Broderick one-quarter Scottish, one-quarter Italian and one-half Jewish. We are also told that Connery's wife was petite, which is the justification for his towering over Hoffman. Connery comments from time to time on how puny his son is, and he is certain that if he had married a Scottish woman Hoffman would be a good five inches taller. Broderick is taller than Hoffman, too, but *that*'s never brought up. (It doesn't make much sense for Connery's character to be Scottish in the first place. Coming to America in 1947, he worked on the piers lining the Hudson River and lived in Hell's Kitchen, which was then a mostly Irish enclave. Twice in the film, "Danny Boy" is sung, but not once do we hear "Loch Lomond.")

Three different profiles, three different noses.

The basic plot of *Family Business* is that Broderick, a restless graduate student bored by middle-class respectability, drops out of M.I.T. and then entices his adored grandfather Connery—a veteran, small-time hood—to be his accomplice on a can't-miss heist. Having served a prison term years earlier, Hoffman turned his back on his father's way of life and has done quite nicely for himself in the meat business; he gets suckered in on the caper because, so he claims, he wants to keep an eye on Broderick. Hoffman blames the family genes for compelling his son to try his luck at a life of crime—he must have seen *The Bad Seed* one too many times. His harping on this point only makes us muse that, if heredity were such a powerful force that it turned Matthew Broderick into a criminal, shouldn't it also have been strong enough to propagate some kind of family resemblance?

Family Business is a mess of a movie that can't decide exactly what it is: boisterous comedy, suspense caper, character study, maudlin soap opera? The film stops and starts in spurts, but you don't notice most of its shortcomings because you're too busy scrutinizing the screen, looking for any shred of evidence to convince you these three men are related. And it's not only the physical dissimilarities that are so distracting; it's voices, too. Connery's Scottish burr has seldom been so pronounced. Meanwhile, Hoffman tries to convey both his character's roots and his current bourgeois existence by modulating his accent between upscale Ted Kramer from *Kramer vs. Kramer* and lowlife Ratso Rizzo from *Midnight Cowboy*. Actingwise, father and son are from two entirely different schools. Hoffman yells and spends much of his time being worked up about something or other. Connery has as many emotional big moments as Hoffman, but, as usual, he underplays them, allowing his natural buoyancy to carry the scene. Hoffman can emote all he wants, but all his tricks will never give him what Sean Connery has: charisma. How one generation can be so charming and the next so irritating?

Broderick doesn't sound like either of the other actors. There's a refinement to his speech, and God only knows how he picked *that* up in this family. His soft-spoken, slightly loopy sweetness lacks the easy authority of Connery but also eschews the pumped-up theatrics of Hoffman. Vocally, he has neither Connery's highland lilt nor the in-your-face directness of Hoffman, but his subdued acting style is much closer to Connery's. The most enjoyable thing about *Family Business* is watching the two low-keyed guys outact the histrionic one with so much ease.

Ava Gardner and Lorne Greene

Earthquake (1974)

"Dada-ism"

Ava Gardner and Lorne Greene, eight years apart in age, would have had no problem passing as husband and wife. But Mark Robson, the producer-director of *Earthquake* had other ideas. Charlton Heston, a year younger than Gardner, was given the role of her spouse. But Greene was in the picture, nonetheless—as Gardner's *father*.

Incomparably beautiful in her twenties and thirties, Gardner was now fifty-one, and looked like a handsome woman in her early to mid fifties. Compared to the "love goddess" she had been dubbed a quarter century earlier, Gardner was undeniably puffier, but, like the craggy Charlton Heston, she simply looked her age. (*Time*'s Richard Schickel wrote, cruelly, that "the camera lingers sadistically on the ruins of a legendary beauty.") The only unnerving thing about her countenance was that, presumably due to a less-than-excellent face-lift, her eyes now had an Asian quality to them.

Lorne Greene was a virile-looking fifty-nine. Sure he had silver hair, but his hair had been gray fifteen years earlier when he began playing Ben Cartwright on *Bonanza* and tried to fool television viewers that he was the pa of three grown sons. Greene didn't look much different from his first appearance on the Ponderosa at age forty-four. To summarize: in *Earthquake*, we're faced with three actors who all appear to be contemporaries though we're told that one of them is at least twenty years older than the other two.

The *Observer* of London didn't get it and commented that as the head of an engineering firm, "Lorne Greene is wheeling and dealing and trying to look like Ava Gardner's father. Unfortunately, there are only eight years

Perhaps the perplexed Charlton Heston is wondering how two people of the same generation can be father and daughter.

between their ages, and not even the cinema's artifice is capable of stretching the gap to a generation's width." In a movie like *Earthquake*, where you enter the theater for two hours of mindless entertainment, you shouldn't be distracted by such unnecessary diversions. *Earthquake*, which was released at the height of the disaster-movie craze, gives the audience exactly what the title promises. The film's main selling point was something called Sensurround—a device that used air vibrations to provide audiences with the less-than-pleasant sensation of actually being in an earthquake. It's a B movie in every aspect other than its budget, and even its cast, other than Heston, Gardner—both past their primes—and Genevieve Bujold, is made up primarily of B-movie veterans: Marjoe, George Kennedy, *Shaft*'s Richard Roundtree, and Gabriel Dell of the *Bowery Boys*.

So why did Mark Robson cast Ava Gardner as Lorne Greene's daughter? Plotwise it wasn't necessary: Heston was a poor boy who came to work at his father-in-law's company, but it could just as well have been his brother-in-law's firm. Much of moviemaking has no rhyme or reason to it, so one could take the easy way out and blame it on that. But if you believe that man is a rational creature, that answer won't do. In *Earthquake*, Heston divides his affection between wife Gardner and winsome Genevieve Bujold (who at thirty-one could credibly have been Greene's daughter—*and* they're both Canadian). Maybe Robson thought he was making a more level playing field for the two women if they seemed closer in age. And if logic told us that any daughter of Lorne Greene would have to be under forty, then maybe he swallowed hard and hoped the audience would dismiss the evidence before them and take Gardner to be in her thirties. (I'm not crazy about this reasoning but I can't do better.)

Bujold *is* a much more desirable catch, but youth has nothing to do with it. Gardner's character, Remy (Lorne Greene must have loved his cognac), is one of the most unremitting shrews ever to be a leading lady. Her initial line in the film is a splenetic "Goddamn it" as she enters the room where Heston is exercising, and vehemently kicks a piece of clothing on the floor. Heston's low-key response: "Your last words last night. The very first words you greet me with this morning. Don't you think you ought to do something about expanding your vocabulary?" This lovely lady's other dialogue includes "If it wasn't seven-thirty in the morning, I would have a drink," "Don't you dare lower your voice to me!" and, short and to the point, "Bastard!" In contrast, the widowed Bujold couldn't be nicer. An aspiring actress with a young son, she is charming, caring, and supportive. When, at the end of the film, Heston forsakes Bujold in order to try to save Gardner (before they are both swept away in a water drain), his choice makes as little sense as the Gardner/Greene casting decision. You have to figure that Heston got discombobulated from the Sensurround.

Dustin Hoffman and Tom Cruise

Rain Man (1988)

"Oh, Brother!"

Rain Man had a tortuous journey to the screen. When Peter Guber and Jon Peters originally optioned the script, they thought it might make a nice little movie with, perhaps, Randy and Dennis Quaid playing on-screen brothers. CAA, the management behemoth, became involved with the project and put together a package that had the unlikely team of Dustin Hoffman and Tom Cruise as the linchpin. When the script's author, Barry Morrow, protested that Cruise was two decades too young for his role, new writers were brought in to replace him. Three A-list directors did preproduction work on *Rain Man* and a series of writers came and went. Finally, Barry Levinson was signed to direct and things got rolling. The mismatching of Hoffman and Cruise was finally going to be put onto celluloid.

While you'd still have a hard time swallowing it, the age difference between the two actors (Hoffman was fifty-one, Cruise twenty-six) could possibly be explained away as the younger man being a "change of life baby." The physical dissimilarities are another story. Dustin Hoffman and Tom Cruise do not have a single feature in common. Look at their body frames, their sizes, their eyes. No way did they have the same parents. And although each boasts a prominent nose, they are differently shaped—Hoffman's wide and long, Cruise's more classically Roman. Neither actor has what you'd call a euphonious voice, but again the two are grating in individual ways. While Hoffman speaks in catarrhal tones—and his standard stutter-whine is more accentuated here because he raises everything up a notch as an autistic man—Cruise's voice is clear but treble, and his speaking style unmodulated.

Dave Kehr of the *Chicago Tribune* cracked that Cruise and Hoffman "seem no more related than Cary Grant and Porky Pig." The filmmakers figured, however, that no one would mind this improbable fraternity too much because it consisted of two major stars. And they weren't wrong: moviegoers turned *Rain Man* into the highest grossing movie of 1988. The worst part is that the two mismatched principals aren't even in a very good movie. Determinedly mediocre, *Rain Man*'s flimsy storyline (Cruise kidnaps the institutionalized autistic brother he never knew about and takes him on a six-day, moneymaking cross-country jaunt) only serves to let the two stars do their standard stuff: Cruise is an immature young man with a nice smile who learns about life and grows up; Hoffman does the attention-grabbing "accomplished" acting that begs for an Academy Award. Which, indeed, he did win.

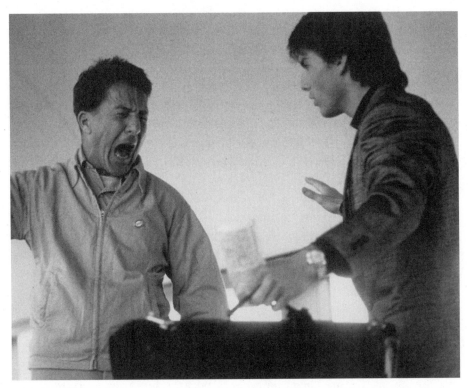

They don't look alike/ They don't sound alike/ You could lose your mind/ When brothers aren't two of a kind.

THE MISCASTING HALL OF FAME

Three actors who, despite undeniable talent and a portfolio of fine performances, also spent a good portion of their careers way over their heads

I have a feeling we're not in the Bronx anymore.

Tony Curtis

The Prince Who Was a Thief (1951)
Son of Ali Baba (1952)
The Black Shield of Falworth (1954)

"Hithah and Yondah"

Tony Curtis developed into a delightful light comedian and, as he got older, a marvelous character actor. His work in *Sweet Smell of Success*, *Some Like It Hot*, *Operation Petticoat*, and, especially, Elia Kazan's *The Last Tycoon* bears witness to "what might have been," if filmmakers had taken better advantage of Curtis's talents over the last two decades. That having been said, it must also be acknowledged that when he was a tyro in the early fifties, Tony Curtis was spectacularly bad.

Curtis was under contract at Universal, a studio that at this point mostly made movies showcasing its roster of fresh-faced, fledgling actors—Rock Hudson, Piper Laurie, Julie Adams—whose skills were mainly decorative. Universal's bill of fare was almost exclusively juvenile, escapism intended for undemanding audiences. (A rule of thumb regarding Universal's fifties films: if it isn't directed by Douglas Sirk, Anthony Mann, or Blake Edwards, it ain't no good. Curtis worked with all three of them, but they had nothing to do with the movies that concern us here.) Along with the *Francis the Talking Mule* and *Ma and Pa Kettle* cash cows, there was a plethora of Westerns, brassy musicals, simplistic melodramas, and Arabian Nights adventures, one of which, *The Prince Who Was a Thief*, gave Tony Curtis his first starring role.

Physically, the swarthy actor does not seem out of place in the Middle East of long ago, except for his pompadour hairdo. But the moment he opens his mouth, he's once again Bernie Schwartz of the Bronx, New York. His hometown dialect renders laughable everything he has to say.

To be young and in love in ancient Baghdad. (Photofest)

Even in a tongue-in-cheek adventure—and this film is nothing if not self-consciously facetious—you want to put some credence in the hero. This is impossible when he sounds like Tony Curtis. Especially Tony Curtis saying a line like "Then I have not found disfavor in your eyes, oh fairest of Islam?"

The Prince Who Was a Thief was allegedly adapted from something that Theodore Dreiser wrote, although, not having read the story, I can't begin to say how it fits into Dreiser's canon of impassioned social realism. (The dead author was having quite a year in Hollywood. First the release of *A Place in the Sun*, adapted from his *An American Tragedy*, and then *this*.) The entire plot of *The Prince Who Was a Thief* is given away in the title: kidnapped as an infant, the young royal is raised by a master thief.

Among the things Curtis hopes to accomplish during the course of the film are breaking into the fortress-like royal treasury to make off with lots of loot, and gaining favor with the local princess by retrieving the pearl that was filched from her. Most of all, though, he wants to reclaim his rightful position as ruler. Looking like a girl who'd be trying out for the cheerleading squad, Piper Laurie is on hand as a fellow thief.

The only things that stand out about *The Prince Who Was a Thief* are the florid insults which dominate the dialogue: "Be gone you sons of she-camels," "Son of a noseless mother! Maggot-brained child of a jackass!" and, from a guard to a gaggle of noisy watch-geese (as in watchdogs), "Son of a rotten egg, what is the matter with you to make noises at night? Quiet, children of a mishatched mother, or instead of filling your bellies, by my sword ye shall fill mine!" (I didn't say they were clever, just that they were conspicuous. These put-downs would indicate that the movie's two scriptwriters had a serious mother-fixation.)

A year later, a movie trailer featured an unctuous narrator rhapsodizing, "By the thousands, your fan letters poured into Hollywood asking us to reteam the two young players you discovered, adored and elevated to stardom! And here they are! Handsome, vigorous, dynamic Tony Curtis! And beautiful and peppery Piper Laurie!" Yes, they were together again, and back where they didn't belong—old Arabia. Plotwise, *Son of Ali Baba* is the same old stuff: as a champion of the downtrodden, Tony takes off his shirt whenever possible and does battle with evil caliph Victor Jory and his equally pernicious son, Hugh O'Brian, while Piper is the Queen of Fez, posing as a fugitive harem girl. If *Son of Ali Baba* is marginally less bad than *The Prince Who Was a Thief*, it's only because it is not as doggedly self-mocking. (There is one genuinely funny element in *Son of Ali Baba*: a pair of deadpan floozies serve as a sort of Greek chorus, making caustic asides ruing the battle of the sexes. To wit, "Men are never fair. But if we're not, we never get any." Later, when the strapping youths of the Royal Military Academy barrel past on their way to battle, the two women futilely try to get their minds on other matters besides war, exclaiming "Here we are, boys! Here we are! Boys! Boys!")

Curtis had made a couple of other films between *The Prince Who Was a Thief*, and *Son of Ali Baba*, and, as a result, he has greater confidence and is a more forceful screen presence this go around. Which doesn't mean that he gives a better performance. He acts with greater gusto, so his Bronx tones are that much more pronounced. For years, Curtis has had to live down the line of dialogue "Yondah lies the castle of my faddah." He said no such thing. His actual line was "This is my faddah's palace, and yondah lies the Valley of the Sun," as he points to a painted background.

Playing a young man named Myles in Olde England, Tony Curtis seemed to be many miles from home.

While Curtis's dark good looks and raven hair minimally offset his vocal incongruities when he cavorted in Arabian Nights pictures, there was no rationalization whatsoever for his participation in a third piece of derring-do from his early years. It's a toss-up as to what's more ridiculous about *The Black Shield of Falworth*, Curtis's rubbing elbows with Henry IV and Prince Hal in fifteenth-century England or simply that he's playing a character named Myles. A peasant lad, he learns that his father was a nobleman who, years earlier, had been falsely accused of treason and put to death. He goes off to learn to become a squire and, in the course of clearing his family's good name, saves the throne for the Henrys and wins the fair hand of his then real-life wife, Janet Leigh.

At times, *The Black Shield of Falworth* plays like a modern-day social tract: Because of his uncultivated background and all-around gaucherie, Tony is taunted and physically assaulted by some of the other guys in his dormitory at squire school. Petulant and moody, he never backs off from a fight back and gains a reputation as a hothead; eventually, he proves himself to be a right proper gentleman. With Curtis's line readings again strictly from the Grand Concourse, it's easy to picture this as a contemporary 1954 film, featuring Tony as a poor lad from a New York slum who receives a scholarship to an Ivy League college where he must overcome the disdain of all the privileged fraternity snobs.

Mostly though, *The Black Shield of Falworth* is simple swashbuckling nonsense, more nonsensical than most because of Curtis's presence. He's still wearing his hair in a pompadour, and how he gets his helmet to fit over that substantial mane is a mystery. *The Black Shield of Falworth* did well at the box office, although his fans may have felt shortchanged: the period fashions didn't accord the actor any opportunities for beefcake shots.

Gregory Peck

Days of Glory (1944)
Captain Horatio Hornblower (1951)
Moby Dick (1956)
Behold a Pale Horse (1964)
The Boys From Brazil (1978)

"Mundane Multinationalist"

Rich in voice, darkly handsome, and an unassailably upright citizen, Gregory Peck is truly an iconographic movie star. No other actor so completely embodies conscience, decency, and the simple compassion that used to epitomize American values until the far right got into the henhouse.

Peck's two most famous films are entreaties for people of goodwill to live up to the ideals of this country. When, in *Gentleman's Agreement*—a movie about a writer who poses as a Jew to get the lowdown on anti-Semitism—Peck says, "words like yid and kike and kikey and nigger and coon make me kind of sick," his conviction is so strong that you feel all the bigots in the world must surely be withering under his stentorian tones. On a purely technical level, Peck's Oscar-winning performance in *To Kill a Mockingbird* is not very accomplished. He plays an attorney in the heart of the Deep South during the 1930s and he doesn't have the slightest trace of a drawl. And yet, because Peck infuses so much probity into the character of Atticus Finch, the defender of a black man falsely accused of rape, his lack of an accent matters not at all. When his material is not as strong, however, or when he's trying to play someone whose sense of moral rectitude is less than impeccable, Peck's disinclination to sound like anyone other than Gregory Peck is jarring. (In *Amazing Grace*

Comrade Peck fights the good fight for Mother Russia against the Germans, but he does take time off from his guerilla duties to romance Tamara Toumanova.

and Chuck, Peck was unconvincing as the president of the United States simply because by 1987 we no longer expected the chief executive to be as upstanding and honest as Gregory Peck.)

Peck's limitations were apparent his very first time out. In *Days of Glory*, he plays the leader of a band of Russian guerrillas fighting the Germans in World War II. Although his leading lady, dancer Tamara Toumanova, speaks with the heavy tones of her native Russia, and the rest of the cast—newcomers culled from radio and the stage—do their best to sound Slavic, Peck opens his mouth and out comes that deep, euphonious voice that would become part of the cultural landscape for over half a century. A very American voice. The actor's stony composure is also already firmly in place, a quality that renders his character's fervor in defending Mother Russia somewhat dubious.

Peck's stiffness and gloomy mien also make his passionate romance with Toumanova a little ridiculous. A ballerina who is entertaining the Russian forces "at Comrade Stalin's behest," she gets caught in the middle of a battle and is separated from civilization. Stumbling across the resistance fighters, Toumanova joins in their guerrilla activities and soon finds herself in Peck's arms. Gregory Peck's laconic style is wildly at odds with such ardent words of love as "Nina, Ninotchka, where do you come from? Your eyes are as wonderful as a forgotten dream." Still, female moviegoers who favored the strong, silent type rallied around the new screen actor; although *Days of Glory* wasn't a hit, Gregory Peck became a hot property. Almost immediately, he developed into one of the biggest names in movies, received four Oscar nominations in a five-year span, and even tried to lighten up from time to time. But he also made a number of missteps, films of varying quality that were all the worse for having starred Gregory Peck.

Peck was at his most inadequate when he tried to force his forthright style onto citizens of other countries. In *Captain Horatio Hornblower*, he impersonates C. S. Forester's British naval captain from the time of the Napoleonic Wars. *Impersonates* is probably not the

Peck indulges in a spot of swashbuckling. The figure next to him is not a ship's masthead but actress Virginia Mayo.

best word, since not a single British pronunciation escapes from his lips. So you grudgingly accept that Hornblower, a citizen of Plymouth in Devon, has an American accent (although if Virginia Mayo—whom nobody would call an actress—can manage a not half-bad job of making herself seem English, Peck could have taken a crack). Peck talking like Peck might not have been as irksome if *Captain Horatio Hornblower* hadn't been filmed in England, its supporting cast made up of very-British local actors.

The Forester book had originally been bought by Warner Bros. with Errol Flynn in mind. Faced with the prospect of now having a less-than-sprightly hero for their swashbuckler, director Raoul Walsh and his writers are never quite sure what to make of Hornblower. In the early segments of the film, he is a humorless disciplinarian ("Hornblower—he ain't human," comments a sailor). This martinet aspect of Hornblower is the one that best suits the actor; Peck's stodginess is not inappropriate for a character who, at this point in the movie, anyway, takes so little pleasure in life.

Throughout the course of *Captain Horatio Hornblower*, Peck never does seem at ease in his early-nineteenth-century British navy regalia, but as the film progresses, Hornblower becomes more "human" (Hornblower is "as gentle and warmhearted as any man who's ever sailed for the King," comments a sailor.) The film takes a tongue-in-cheek turn once Virginia Mayo—as the Duke of Wellington's sister!—comes aboard ship and, trying to get into the spirit, Peck engages in a good deal of throat-clearing, coughing, and hemming and hawing. Fun is supposed to arise from the fact that "no one's ever seen Hornblower speak to a lady," but the stolid virtue of Gregory Peck doesn't blend with self-effacement, and this attempt at humor might make you wince. He lacks, shall we say, a light touch. (*Time* groused that Peck "looks, acts and sounds more like a junior Lincoln than a British sea dog.")

Hornblower and Lady Barbara fall in love, but when Virginia Mayo breathlessly tells him, "I don't want this voyage to end. . . . You must know it. I love you. Why do you fight against it?" that romantic fool Gregory Peck responds with a stammer. He adds, "I'm married." She's not free herself, having become engaged to a crusty admiral, but Peck and Mayo do get in some nuzzling, giving him the opportunity to sound foolish murmuring, "Barbara, Barbara." When Hornblower returns home to Plymouth, however, he receives good news: his wife has died in childbirth. (Obviously, Mayo's admiral is going to get killed in battle, clearing the way for a happy ending.)

Before Peck and Mayo can have a fade-out clinch, there are stubborn superior officers to butt heads with, ocean battles to fight, and enemy soldiers to kill. The actor also gets in a moment of full-throttled emoting when he's interrogating a captured French captain who's giving him the runaround. "C'mon, man, or I'll guillotine you here and now!" he screams through clenched teeth, and it strikes you that Peck being dull and lifeless is not as bad as Peck trying to be hot-tempered.

Even Peck's *leg* is not as wooden as his performance as Captain Ahab. (Museum of Modern Art/Film Stills Archives)

This a problem for John Huston's version of *Moby Dick*, in which Peck plays Captain Ahab. You might argue that it would take someone with a very vivid imagination to think of stalwart, noble Gregory Peck in conjunction with the man who had the world's biggest chip on his shoulder. In reality, it wasn't imagination, it was the desire to make a buck. Huston couldn't get financial backing for the film when he told potential investors that Fredric March or Orson Welles would make a swell Ahab. But having Gregory Peck on the marquee, that was different: Peck was money in the bank at the time and who cares that he was two decades too young for the role. For all of his largely self-generated image as a supreme Hollywood iconoclast, Huston was willing to compromise his vision and said "fine." (The director had first written a *Moby Dick* script in 1946 and hoped to cast his now-deceased father, Walter Huston. Warner Bros. announced in 1949 that the film would be on its production slate, most likely with Errol Flynn starring. Other names that came up in discussions among studio brass at the time were Gary Cooper, Burt Lancaster, John Wayne, and . . . Gregory Peck.) When the movie finally got a green light in 1955, Peck claimed he was surprised to be offered the role because of the age discrepancy between himself and the character. Besides, he envisioned himself more as a Starbuck type (the chief mate who was eventually played by British actor Leo Genn).

Hundreds of thousands of pages in master's theses have been expended discussing the inherent meanings and symbolism of every character, piece of action, and inanimate object found in the pages of Herman Melville's broodingly theosophical novel. For our purposes we'll just concentrate on the character that Gregory Peck plays. Melville writes of Ahab: "He looked like a man cut away from the stake, when the fire has overrunningly wasted all the limbs without consuming them or taking away one particle from their comparted aged robustness." It's doubtful that a studio biography would have described Gregory Peck as such.

Peck bellows, snarls, and throws ear-splitting fits of pique. But these are all surface effects, and when Ahab is not carrying on about the white whale, Peck plays him not as a man consumed with rage but simply as a stern sea captain; except for the beard and muttonchops, this could be a redux of Horatio Hornblower. When Peck and Leo Genn's Starbuck have a row over the captain's orders, the point of reference is more *Mutiny on the Bounty* than Melville. Paraphrasing Melville, Richard Basehart's Ishmael says that Ahab possesses "the marks of some inner crucifixion and woe deep in his veins." But we have our own visual evidence and can see that Gregory Peck isn't like that all: he's simply testy. Squinting his eyes and glaring for long stretches of time, Peck, at most, appears to be having a very genteel nervous breakdown.

Peck couldn't escape comparisons with our sixteenth president; Bosley Crowther of the *New York Times* wrote that the actor "gives Ahab a towering, gaunt appearance that is markedly Lincolnesque." At times Peck also resembles his director, and the similarity makes you realize that John Huston would have been a more effective vengeance-obsessed madman than his star. Peck himself felt so and stated that Huston's "intense desire to make this picture without any compromise is certainly comparable to Ahab's relentless quest to kill the whale." No matter how hard a filmmaker may try to turn Melville into cinematic high art—and Huston and screenwriter Ray Bradbury were certainly trying for that, with myriad

The beret is a nice, jaunty touch, but it can't compensate for Peck's lack of an accent as a Republican veteran of the Spanish Civil War.

biblical references spelled out for slower viewers—a film version of *Moby Dick* is destined to remain an adventure film. Peck later said, "I'm not sure that *Moby Dick* can be done at all. I saw both previous versions with John Barrymore, and they were perfectly awful, too."

In *Behold a Pale Horse*, in which he plays a former leader of Republican Forces in the Spanish Civil War, Peck has two obstacles to mount and fails both of them. As Artiguez, who has been exiled in France for twenty years but makes periodic raids into his homeland, Peck has to be an impassioned man of the people; it would also be to the film's advantage if he convinced us that he's Spanish. A supposedly legendary figure, Artiguez is, in conception, as much a force of nature as a human being. In real life, Peck would undoubtedly be very capable of engaging in well-reasoned, intellectual discussions on the virtues of the Spanish anti-Fascists, but conveying the pride, the anger, and the blind determination of one such person is beyond him. Ironically, Anthony Quinn, who plays his nemesis, a corrupt Fascist police chief, has the intense fury Peck can't seem to bring to his character.

When he speaks, Peck's Spanish guerrilla fighter sounds much like his Russian guerrilla fighter from *Days of Glory*. Peck's production company made *Behold a Pale Horse*, but, in his role as producer, he didn't insist that his star try for vocal authenticity. He does make one small effort at essaying a characterization. Artiguez has been fighting the good fight for two decades and is growing weary of life; Peck, therefore, tinges his commanding voice with a slight touch of gruffness. His dialect, though, remains firmly entrenched in the States. He also wears a beret, but that could mark him as French as much as Spanish, so we'll call that attempt a draw.

Directed by Fred Zinnemann, *Behold a Pale Horse* is a pointedly symbolic political drama featuring the good left (Peck), the bad right (Quinn), and the innocent apolitical (Omar Sharif, as a priest who becomes involved in a final showdown between the two sides). The film is way too schematic to be effective, and because Quinn's and Sharif's performances are so much more persuasive than Peck's, the balance of power shifts in a way that wasn't intended. It deserves points for earnestness, if nothing else. The movie bombed everywhere, save for portions of the Middle East (where throngs always came out to see favorite son Omar Sharif). And Franco's government was so incensed by *Behold a Pale Horse* that for years it wouldn't allow Columbia to release any films in Spain.

Gregory Peck as Dr. Josef Mengele? Having represented the positive in human nature for so long, Peck clearly relished playing one of the most evil people who ever lived—in *The Boys From Brazil* he manages to make himself speak with a pronounced German accent. His Mengele is a blowhard who snarls and sneers and flies into hyperkinetic rages—all in all a fairly stereotypical version of the "Teutonic Hun." (Magazine articles about *The Boys From Brazil* couldn't resist referring to this character as "Peck's Bad Boy.") His skin is drained of all color and his hair and mustache looks to have been smeared with black shoe polish, but he can't bamboozle us. This is still that paragon of morality, Gregory Peck. Despite all his bombastic activity, Peck is unable to divest himself of his trademark sonorous tones, and manages to sound only like an impressionist at a Munich nightclub doing Gregory Peck. (Peck's German shadings also recall the actor John Banner's Sgt. Schultz on *Hogan's Heroes*.)

If Peck's work as the notorious Nazi medical experimenter is less than convincing, that's okay: It's still a kick to hear *Gregory Peck* screaming,

Nice guy Peck's wacky over-the-top acting as the vile Dr. Josef Mengele might be considered "Mein Camp."

"He betrayed me! He betrayed you! He betrayed the Aryan race!" Besides, *The Boys From Brazil* is not something that needs to be taken seriously. A superfluous but not unentertaining movie, *The Boys From Brazil* is all about Mengele's having cloned ninety-four little versions of Adolf Hitler. (Der Fuehrer allowed Mengele "to take half a liter of his blood and a cutting of skin from his ribs" for this purpose.)

When *The Boys From Brazil* begins, the cloning process is at the stage where the junior Hitlers are young teenagers and, in order to replicate the life of the real man, Mengele has given the command that all of their adoptive fathers are to be killed, just as Hitler's father died when he was an adolescent. Laurence Olivier pops up as a Simon Wiesenthal clone traveling the globe to stop the murders. With his Austrian accent and fussbudgety movements, Olivier is every bit as hammy as Peck, and a highlight is their climactic showdown, in which the two oldtimers end up rolling around on the floor trying to kill each other. The best moment comes shortly after, as Peck is to trying to convince one of his creations to murder Olivier. In the midst of cajoling the youth, Peck giddily tells him "You're Adolf Hitler!" To which the boy calmly responds, "Oh, man, you're weird." This was the first time in Gregory Peck's career that somebody could say such a thing and be telling the truth.

Frank Sinatra

The Miracle of the Bells (1948)
The Kissing Bandit (1948)
Johnny Concho (1956)
The Pride and the Passion (1957)
Can-Can (1960)

"I Did It My Way!"

Most people would tell you that Frank Sinatra was the most sublime of all pop singers, and they'd get no argument from me (even if Johnny Hartman did have more class). On the other hand, nobody would seriously claim Sinatra was the greatest of actors (or even among, say, the top 250). Still, he has from time to time been awfully good in the movies. While Sinatra's Oscar-winning performance in *From Here to Eternity* was notable more for raising his career from the dead than for any thespian wonders, he's very likable in that film. He was especially impressive as an emotionally withdrawn writer in *Some Came Running* and especially gutsy as a junkie in *The Man With the Golden Arm*. (Then there were all those "clan" movies in which, essentially, he just hung around with Dino and Sammy and Peter and Joey while the cameras rolled. But that's another story.)

One of the astonishing things about Sinatra as a singer was how adept and precise he was with every possible mood and attitude: the cocky swinger, the hopeless romantic, the cool hipster, the visionary dreamer, the unabashed pietist, the sympathetic bearer of wisdom and good cheer. Contrarily, Sinatra's range as an actor was markedly limited. When a film called upon him to be self-absorbed or insolent, things were generally fine, but sincerity and modesty were problems. Playing in period pieces

Bless me, faddah. Neither Frank Sinatra nor Fred
MacMurray appears terribly interested in MacMurray's sad
tale. (Museum of Modern Art/Film Stills Archives)

and portraying characters who were not from the greater New York met-
ropolitan area likewise did not come easily.

Not counting the 1945 short film, *The House I Live In*—in which he
lectured a group of neighborhood bullies about tolerance and brotherhood—*The Miracle of the Bells* was Sinatra's first dramatic acting role.
It did not bode well. *The Miracle of the Bells* is one of the damnedest
things ever to come out of Hollywood. Based on a critically lambasted
novel that became a huge bestseller (the *Bridges of Madison County* of
1946) this treacly melodrama is about—listen carefully—a miracle that
allows a shelved movie to be released. Told in flashbacks, *The Miracle of
the Bells* is framed by Hollywood press agent Bill Dunnigan's (Fred Mac-
Murray) journey to return the body of actress Olga Treskovna (Alida
Valli) for burial in her hometown (picturesquely called "Coaltown, Pennsylvania"). The dead woman is an unknown, but it shouldn't have been

that way, and Dunnigan, who was smitten with her, knows that better than anyone else.

Olga had struggled for years, performing in crummy burlesque houses in jerkwater towns before finally landing the lead in a Hollywood movie about Joan of Arc. (She had been born Olga Trocki, but that would never do for a stage name so she became Treskovna.) The actress gives a brilliant performance, but then she has to go and die the day after the production wraps. Studio head Marcus Harris (Lee J. Cobb) is not about to release a film with a dead unknown in it, and never mind how Oscar-worthy her performance is—it'd be too much of a downer for moviegoers. So while making funeral arrangements, Dunnigan concocts an angle for getting *Joan of Arc* into theaters. He pays the five Catholic churches in Coaltown to ring their bells nonstop for three days in honor of Olga. With a press agent's acumen, he figures the wire services will pick up on all the racket, and every newspaper in the country will then feature a story on both the clanging bells and the dead actress who inspired them. And the publicity will give the studio no choice but to release *Joan of Arc*. The tintinnabulation *does* receive nationwide attention, but movie mogul Harris remains obdurate.

Frank Sinatra is Father Paul, the pastor of St. Michael's, the poorest of the parishes; as a local snob says, "nobody worthwhile goes there . . . Just miners." Which means, of course, that Father Paul is entirely unassuming and unaffected. While appropriate for a sincere young priest, these qualities do not hang well on Frank Sinatra. Portraying this humble man of faith, Sinatra is subdued—virtually in a trance. He says his lines hesitatingly, almost phonetically, and his speaking voice is both soft and surprisingly high-pitched, qualities that make him a most feeble screen presence. The good priest is at his most sensitive when speaking of the women of Coaltown: "The sins of the poor lie in their poverty, not themselves." It's probable that back in 1948—when he was an impassioned liberal—Sinatra believed these words. But that doesn't mean he could say them on-screen with much conviction. (His performance points out a contrast between Sinatra the vocalist and Sinatra the actor: he has made recordings of spirituals and religious Christmas songs that are heartfelt, pure, and altogether beautiful. Hearing them, you'd think he was someone who'd spent his whole life in church.)

At one point, Father Paul is trying his hardest to be forceful and intimidating while talking to an unscrupulous undertaker. In real life, Sinatra was already famously brawling with newspaper columnists, so this scene featured a tough guy pretending to be a milquetoast pretending to be a tough guy—it's a bizarrely incongruous amalgam of the meek and the macho.

So what about the film's eponymous miracle? Well, while Father Paul is officiating at Olga's funeral, statues of the Blessed Mother and St. Michael the Archangel come to life—they've turned toward Olga's casket. What a development! There is, however, a logical explanation for the sculptures' curiosity: Father Paul discovers that the weight of all the mourners in the church caused the ground below to shift, thus tilting the statues.

But never give a sucker an even break. Nowadays some people are convinced that the Virgin Mary has made appearances on a screen door in Bayside, Queens—though of all the places in the world she could visit, why there?—and a few years back there were reported sightings of Jesus on a billboard for spaghetti sauce someplace down South. So who's to say that back in the late forties, a lot of people wouldn't have chosen to believe that a couple of marble statues really did want to sneak a peak at the coffin. Delighted at seeing everyone suddenly get that old-time religion, Father Paul is not about to burst their bubble, not with his little church turning into a holy shrine—a coal region version of Lourdes.

And Dunnigan's wish comes true: Because of the heavenly intercession, Olga will be seen on movie screens everywhere and her genius recognized by the whole world. Lest this miracle seem overly secular and too far removed from the realm of the sacred, the movie allows us to become privy to Olga's deathbed speech, where she proclaims that she didn't desire fame and fortune for herself. No, Olga selflessly wanted to be in movies for the "poor, sad people" of Coaltown because "I came out of them. When they hear me, they'll know it's their own hearts speaking. When they see my name shining in all the theaters, it will be something of theirs shining." Nice try, lady, but you're the one who'd be getting the limousine and driver, the mansion and house staff, and all the other trappings of Hollywood stardom. Those poor schmoes will still be stuck in Coaltown, and if I know human nature, they're going to be consumed with envy, not good cheer.

Sinatra had a better rapport with his horse than with leading lady Kathryn Grayson. (Museum of Modern Art/Film Stills Archives)

Altogether terrible, *The Miracle of the Bells* is undeniably fascinating in its awfulness. When it's all over, you simply can't believe that the film turns out to be nothing more than a sanctimonious ode to the power and the glory of the publicity agent. Frank Sinatra's performance is thoroughly in keeping with the utter artificiality of the movie. It's remarkable how an actor trying so hard to be sincere can come off so phony.

His next release (although it was filmed first), *The Kissing Bandit*, is merely awful. Sinatra plays curly-haired Ricardo, the son of a legendary thief in nineteenth-century California whose trademark was bussing women after he robbed them; they fell into such swoons that they didn't mind losing their material possessions to him. Ricardo, on the other hand, is a bashful young man who has just returned from innkeeper's school in Boston and whose goal in life is to create the best hotel on the West Coast. His late father's cronies persuade him to pick up where his old man left off, which he does up to a point—he'll steal, but he's too much of a gentleman to kiss women to whom he has not been formally introduced. Pouty Kathryn Grayson, the daughter of the governor, obsesses over the fact that she did not receive a kiss after being robbed, thinking herself unappealing and not realizing that her bandit was second generational. And so it goes.

A would-be Zorro spoof, this musical fails on almost every count, beginning with its star. In a movie parody, the audience should be able to visualize the lead actor in a serious version of the story. The alarmingly gaunt Frank Sinatra would never have been cast as a dashing rogue of the Old West, so there's no possible fun to be had watching him kid the conventions of the genre. Plus, he's just plain bad in the film. The humor in *The Kissing Bandit* is supposed to arise from Ricardo's lack of panache. But as Sinatra plays him, he's not merely sheepish, he's downright imbecilic. (Over the decades, Sinatra never did develop into a farceur of any skill.)

Ricardo has a number of attributes that were all wrong for Sinatra. This is another self-effacing character, and Sinatra's no better at diffidence here than in *The Miracle of the Bells*. In addition, you're supposed to believe that Sinatra has never kissed a woman before—even the most naive bobby-soxer would have had trouble swallowing that one. And

although one shouldn't be a stickler for authenticity with movies like this you'd hope that Ricardo might at least talk like, say, Ricardo Montalban, who has a dance number in the film; Sinatra instead brings the sound of Hoboken to Old California. Moreover, there's something off-balance about a film in which the leading lady is heftier than the hero. Many years later, Kathryn Grayson recounted, "I did everything I could to get out of kissing Frank Sinatra in the film, because he was so thin I thought he had some disease. I was afraid I might catch it!" Frank Sinatra's evaluation: "Was *The Kissing Bandit* the nadir of my career? Hell, it was the nadir of *anybody's* career."

Sinatra next put on Western duds in *Johnny Concho* in 1956. A lot had transpired in the years since *The Kissing Bandit*.

Talk about having to suspend your disbelief: this skinny fellow is the terror of Cripple Creek, Arizona. (Museum of Modern Art/Film Stills Archives)

The box-office failures of that film and *The Miracle of the Bells* were matched by a precipitous drop in the popularity of Sinatra's records, marking a career decline that lasted for a half-decade. It was *From Here to Eternity* that fueled his spectacular reemergence as a top star, which coincided with a ripening of his singing voice and a maturing of his presentation. Such records as "Young at Heart" and the *Songs for Young Lovers* album proved irresistible: heartfelt and insinuating, they were a refreshing tonic against the belters whose bombast had been dominating the charts. Sinatra also self-consciously began cultivating his image as a "swinger." Projecting a seminal persona for the mid-fifties, he became a role model for millions of American males as an embodiment of the Cyrenaic philosophy of *Playboy*—the magazine Hugh Hefner launched in 1953, the same year that *From Here to Eternity* was released.

Sinatra was bigger than he had ever been and one of Hollywood's top box-office draws. (In 1955 alone, he had five movies in release.) Befitting his position, he joined the increasing number of actors who produced their own films. His initial foray was *Johnny Concho*. As opposed to *The Kissing Bandit*, this time when he headed out west he wasn't fooling around. Which may be why *Johnny Concho* is so much funnier a film. How come an Italian guy from New Jersey would put himself in a Western? One can only surmise that it was a combination of arrogance—back on top of the world, Sinatra felt he could get away with anything—and wish-fulfillment—urban kids went to cowboy movies, too. Once he had decided on a horse opera, it's surprising that he would have picked this particular one as a vehicle: *Johnny Concho* is a peculiar Western in which Sinatra gave himself an exceptionally unheroic role to play.

Johnny Concho is cowardly and weak (not to mention scrawny—Sinatra looks like a child's stick-figure drawing), yet the entire populace of Cripple Creek, Arizona, is in mortal fear of him and kowtows to his every whim. This anomaly stems from Johnny's dumb luck—Arizona's number one gunslinger happens to be his brother. Although he doesn't live in Cripple Creek, Red Concho is indeed his brother's keeper; one word from Johnny and it'd be curtains for anyone foolish enough to give him offense. As the local judge concedes, "We're a weak and weary flock."

The townspeople's degree of servility is illustrated by a game of poker that takes on absurdist proportions: Johnny declares himself the winner of every round, and the other players acquiesce without a peep—even though Johnny never shows the cards he's holding (giving new meaning to the term "liar's poker"). As an example of a game having existential overtones, it's right up there with the chess match against Death in *The Seventh Seal* a year later.

By and by, brother Red gets his, and the locals are liberated. Frightened by Johnny no longer, they take advantage of their newfound freedom by being rude to him. Their liberty is short-lived: there's a new and more ornery bully in town, one Tallman (William Conrad), the varmint who rubbed out Red. Tallman wants to have a go at Johnny as well, but the poltroon frantically skedaddles out of town when his former toadies (not unreasonably) scoff at his pleas for help. Since we know that Frank Sinatra has never backed down from a fight—and has started more than a few in his time—the sight of him sissified and groveling before William Conrad is even more amusing than seeing him astride a horse and wearing a ten-gallon hat.

Posters for *Johnny Concho* promised that "The Screen's Hottest Star Turns On the Heat in His First Western!" but it was a bust with the public and the critics. (The *Hollywood Reporter* chuckled that "some of the dialogue seems to be more indigenous to Toots Shor's than to the Cripple Creek saloon.") Obviously influenced by *High Noon*, *Johnny Concho* is low-key, talky, and dull. Although somber in style, the film is awfully silly in execution. As any Western starring Frank Sinatra was bound to be.

Even more implausible than Frank Sinatra playing a cowboy—who at least was a United States citizen—was Frank Sinatra playing a Spanish guerrilla fighter, circa 1810. Stanley Kramer's interminable *The Pride and the Passion* is literally a movie about moving a cannon. Sinatra is Miguel, the leader of a band of Spanish patriots who are transporting the huge weapon cross-country so that it can be used against Napoleon's forces. Also on hand are Cary Grant as a captain from the British Royal Navy who wants the cannon for the English when Miguel's gang is through with it; and Sophia Loren as a hot-blooded wench whose main function in terms of plot is to cause jealous friction between her two male costars, but whose bottom-line purpose was to lure male moviegoers into theaters with her low-cut peasantwear.

Sophia Loren, Frank Sinatra, and Cary Grant can't convince us that they belong in Spain during the Napoleonic Wars. They probably couldn't convince themselves either.

The Pride and the Passion is filled with discussions about the best strategies for relocating the damned weapon, along with palaver about the meaning of patriotism and loyalty, but mostly the film consists of scene after scene of the cannon being moved. This makes for less-than-compelling viewing, despite the occasional mishaps that befall the artillery along the way—crashing down a mountain, getting stuck in the mud. So your mind gets to wandering, and you wonder how the gun can be so large and the Spaniards so noisy and yet Napoleon's troops so oblivious to their presence. And you contemplate how this cannon is just about the most obvious phallic symbol imaginable and wonder why that quality doesn't serve any purpose in the movie.

Sinatra uses a Spanish accent that is pure José Jimenez ("jew" for "you"). He also lacks the coarseness you'd reasonably expect to find in this uneducated and volatile man of the people. Miguel was yet another Sinatra role that called for him to be humble, and the most he can manage is a slouching of the shoulders. Another question that crosses your mind in its wanderings is, What was Sinatra thinking when he agreed to wear such an unbecoming toupee with wispy bangs plastered on his forehead?

Sinatra's Spanish accent was far from convincing in *The Pride and the Passion*, but he did make an attempt. In *Can-Can*, an inelegant musical very loosely based on the Cole Porter Broadway hit, he plays a fin de siècle Parisian bon vivant, but he's really playing Frank Sinatra, circa 1960. The movie takes place in the cafes and dance halls of Montmartre but it might as well be set in the Sands Hotel.

Can-Can owed its existence at least in part to the success of *Gigi*, and Louis Jourdan and Maurice Chevalier from the earlier Parisian movie are on hand here, too. Except for costar Shirley MacLaine (who is astonishingly shrill in the one bad performance of her career), everyone surrounding Sinatra speaks in Gallic-flavored English, making Sinatra's insistence on sounding like himself seem all the more lazy and contemptuous of his audience. (Though, admirably, when a French word does come up—a street address—he pronounces it perfectly acceptably, like a second-year high school French student.) Sinatra is so anachronistic as to saddle the song "C'est Magnifique" with the phrase "ring-a-ding-ding," his terminology of choice back then to express a devil-may-care attitude. Bosley Crowther of the *New York Times* felt that Sinatra and MacLaine were like "companions in a Hoboken bar, slightly intoxicated and garrulous with gags. The experience of watching and listening to two such people would probably be as amusing as watching and listening to Mr. Sinatra and Miss MacLaine."

The gist of *Can-Can* is the scandal caused by the illegal title dance, which was, in fact, never outlawed in Paris (although it was banned in London). The movie was meant to be racy and naughty and to that end is filled with heavy-handed innuendos. "This is my boudoir," says MacLaine to Louis Jourdan. "It's also my office. I do most of my work here." And in discussing how one's name reveals nothing about a person's character, Sinatra remarks, "I even knew a girl who called herself Virginia." He does have a point about the irrelevance of names, though. Despite playing himself, Sinatra's moniker in the film is "François."

Index